MW01701386

The Holy Spirit. Our Gift, our Guide.

Who He is and why we need Him according to God's Word.

The Holy Spirit. Our Gift, our Guide.

Who He is and why we need Him according to God's Word.

Marco Harris

Paperback published by Marco Harris 2024

First edition
Paperback ISBN: 979-8-9869587-0-5
E-book ISBN: 978-0-692-98815-2

Editing by Evan Benjamin

This one is for You Holy Spirit.
This one is for You.

Table of Contents

Acknowledgement

I dedicate the following book to the one Being and the two people who planted the seeds and made this book a reality. First, I want to thank the Holy Spirit for inspiring, equipping and empowering me. I wrote this book to help others learn more about You, but in doing so, I learned so much about You. You've inspired me in so many ways, and I love Your presence in my life. I hope that everyone who reads this book will desire a more intimate and powerful walk with You as I have. I love you and I will be forever grateful for everything that you are to me.

Secondly, I would like to thank my parents for being my champions and two of my strongest supporters. Thank you, Dad, for being on my team since day one. Thank you for your love and your guidance. Thank you for being a shining example of what a father should be. Thank you, Mom, for being a vessel that the Spirit uses to touch many lives. Your walk is not one for accolades or fanfare, rather, you just simply want to serve and set captives free. I know the walk has not been easy, but you've blessed me with your perseverance and your line in the sand. Because of you, I began to see that the Spirit was more than His gift of tongues…He is a guide who is ready to work through a willing and committed vessel.

Finally, I want to thank my beautiful wife Morgan for encouraging me through this process and being the vessel that God knew I needed. It is wonderful to be in love with someone who is on one accord with me in the Spirit, and who shares a passion for both God and people. That is only one of the many things that I love about you.

I.

Prologue

1

Prologue (Letter to the Holy Spirit)

Dear Holy Spirit,

I remember the first time I experienced Your "pull" when I was eight years old. At that age, I had no idea who You were, but You tugged through my gut (John 7:38,39) as my pastor gave the congregation an invitation to discipleship. I answered Your tug. I arose, went to the front of the church and sat in the front pew with a sense of anticipation. I could not explain it, but I knew that I needed to give my life to God. On the day I arose from the watery depths of the baptismal pool, I did so as a new man. I had no idea that my baptism would set the stage for a beautiful and fulfilling relationship with God and You.

After I accepted Your invitation, I studied my little children's King James Bible and answered the many questions I had about God. When my family joined another ministry, the new surroundings encouraged me to ask and answer more questions. This transition heightened my desire to learn more about the depths of God.

One Sunday morning, the pastor delivered a message about You, and it piqued my curiosity. At the end of the service, the pastor posed a question to the congregation. He asked if anyone wanted Your gift of speaking in tongues (1 Corinthians 14). The pastor always posed this question after every service, but this time, I felt another "pull" that came from that familiar place (John 7:38). I raised my hand, stood up and headed to the altar. I remember being the only one at the altar that day, but I did not care. My spirit was hungry, and I lost any thought of being embarrassed.

So, on that day, at the age of thirteen, I went to the altar and received Your gift of speaking in tongues through prayer and the laying on of hands. (Acts 2:4, 1 Corinthians 12:10, 1 Corinthians 14)

The infilling and the gift spurred an excitement and an energy to my life in Christ. My thirst for spiritual knowledge and praise and worship increased. I began to read more about You, the spiritual world and spiritual warfare.

I also had the advantage of growing up in a home where we were encouraged to have a personal relationship with God. You gave my mother a strong spiritual gift set, and I learned so much from her example. As children, my brother, sister and I were always "encouraged" to go to church (which meant that we did not have a choice), but even though we were "encouraged," each of us chose to have an engaging relationship with God. One day, my mother gave us "Good Morning, Holy Spirit" by Pastor Benny Hinn. Reading this book at the age of seventeen was a game changer for my spiritual walk. After reading the book, I wanted to know You beyond the gift of tongues. I wanted to know You as my friend and guide.

During my senior year in high school, our youth pastor asked us if we wanted to go to a youth conference sponsored by Pastor Hinn's church. He often spoke about You as a person, and I brought a high level of expectation with me as we drove south to Orlando.

By the end of the conference, there was a shift in my walk. I began to talk to and engage You more. I began to ask You for guidance, discernment and any anything else You were willing to give me. My relationship with You grew in ways that it had not before. Even now I am at a place where I know there is still more to discover, and my goal is to be Your Isaiah 61:1 vessel that binds broken hearts and preaches good tidings to the meek.

I thank you so much for Your gift of You, and I appreciate Your patience as I work hard every day for You to be my Leader. I pray that this book gives readers an opportunity to learn more about You and discover Your desire to guide and empower them. I love you and look forward to every new step we take together.

Love,
Your servant,
Marco

II.

Introduction

2

Introduction (Letter to the Reader)

Dear Reader:

I know that some of you may ask why this "random guy" would write a book about the Holy Spirit. This book evolved from a bible study meant for someone who had questions about the Holy Spirit and questioned His relevance in our Christian walk. This book was the best way that I could express my love of and passion for the Holy Spirit to someone who had no idea who the Spirit was. As I compiled the review, I discovered more about the Holy Spirit's character and what He longs to share with us.

I have been in churches where there was little to no mention of the Holy Spirit. I have been in churches where members met the topic of the Holy Spirit with terse and dismissive responses. Other churches simplified the conversation on the Holy Spirit by only alluding to the gift of speaking in tongues.

With "*The Holy Spirit. Our Gift, our Guide*," I want to use the Word of God and show you what He can be and wants to be to you. As Christians, we should engage the person of the Holy Spirit on a daily basis. If He was sent to us to be our guide (John 16:13), we should talk to him, spend time with Him, and consult Him. I am the first to admit that there are places and spaces that I need to go with the Holy Spirit.

Leaning on the Holy Spirit is not always easy as this walk requires a dedicated and persistent faith with a strong dose of humility and submission.

As you read this book I want you to know that the Holy Spirit is a promise to you as He is for anyone else (Acts 2:39). God is no respecter of persons (Acts 10:34). The Holy Spirit is not meant for a few, but for us all. Invite the Holy Spirit in, spend time with Him and let Him nourish you with everything He is. As the Holy Spirit has been with me, He is always ready to lend everything He can to you and your walk. Romans tells us that the earth cries out for the sons of God who are led by the Spirit (Romans 8: 14,19)

I entitled the book "*The Holy Spirit. Our Gift, our Guide*," because I want every reader to know that the Holy Spirit uses the Word He inspired to let us know what He brings to our lives. He wants to empower every Christian (if we allow Him to) and remove the veil of mystery to many. Throughout the Bible (and this book) you will notice the Holy Spirit mentioned in the following ways:

- Holy Spirit
- Holy Ghost
- Spirit
- Spirit of the Lord
- Spirit of God

I will reference Him as the Holy Spirit to maintain a level of consistency. There is no theological reason behind this selection and nothing more than light preference. I usually call Him "H" (which He responds to), but I promise you that I will maintain a place of formality.

For those who may not know the Holy Spirit or want to know more about Him, my prayer is that you will be able to discover and receive what you need to have as you read this book. I wanted you to have rapid access to biblical information on the Spirit so that you would know who you are calling upon and that you can quickly use this information in your ministry, your prayers and in your walk with God.

That being said, in love, I give you, "The Holy Spirit. Our Gift, our Guide."

Your friend in Christ,
Marco Harris

All passages are from the King James Version of the Bible. All Greek definitions are from The New Thayer's Greek-English Lexicon.

III.

The Holy Spirit in the Old Testament

3

The Holy Spirit in the Old Testament (Letter)

Dear Holy Spirit:

I have always heard that the Old Testament foreshadows Christ. As I compiled this study, I learned that Christ is not the only one the Bible introduces in Old Testament. Whenever I wanted to read about You, I would skip over the Old Testament and promptly head to the New Testament. At times, I wondered if You ever showed up in the Old Testament.

My surprise came when I found out just how active You were in the Old Testament. I knew the stories of Gideon, Samson, and Joshua. I knew that they followed God. I knew that they were victorious in their respective ways, but I did not know that You were in Gideon's victory (Judges 6:34), Samson's strength (Judges 13: 24,25) and Joshua's way (Deuteronomy 34:9, Numbers 27:18).

Further study showed that not only did You use the "popular" characters of the Old Testament, but You also moved on "little guys" like Othniel (Judges 3:10), Jephthah (Judges 11:29), Medad (Numbers 11:26), and so forth. Your use of multiple vessels showed me that You are not a respecter of persons and that You desire to share everything You are with those who are ready to embrace you.

My prayer is that as the reader works through Your Old Testament revelation, that You will begin to show them the great things that are to come.

Love,
Your Servant,
Marco

4

The Holy Spirit in the Old Testament (Scriptures)

He facilitates acknowledgment/respect from others

Daniel 4:8: But at the last Daniel came in before me, whose name was Belteshazzar, according to the name of my god, and in whom is the spirit of the holy gods: and before him I told the dream, saying,

Daniel 4:9: O Belteshazzar, master of the magicians, because I know that the spirit of the holy gods is in thee, and no secret troubleth thee, tell me the visions of my dream that I have seen, and the interpretation thereof.

Daniel 4:18: This dream I king Nebuchadnezzar have seen. Now thou, O Belteshazzar, declare the interpretation thereof, forasmuch as all the wise men of my kingdom are not able to make known unto me the interpretation: but thou art able; for the spirit of the holy gods is in thee.

Daniel 5:11: There is a man in thy kingdom, in whom is the spirit of the holy gods; and in the days of thy father light and understanding and wisdom, like the wisdom of the gods, was found in him; whom the king Nebuchadnezzar thy father, the king, I say, thy father, made master of the magicians, astrologers, Chaldeans, and soothsayers;

Daniel 5:14: I have even heard of thee, that the spirit of the gods is in thee, and that light and understanding and excellent wisdom is found in thee.

He encourages agreement/alignment

1 Chronicles 12:18: Then the spirit came upon Amasai, who was chief of the captains, and he said, Thine are we, David, and on thy side, thou son of Jesse: peace, peace be unto thee, and peace be to thine helpers; for thy God helpeth thee. Then David received them, and made them captains of the band.

He kindles (righteous) anger

1 Samuel 11:6: And the Spirit of God came upon Saul when he heard those tidings, and his anger was kindled greatly.

He anoints kings

Saul

1 Samuel 10:6: And the Spirit of the LORD will come upon thee, and thou shalt prophesy with them, and shalt be turned into another man.

David

1 Samuel 16:13: Then Samuel took the horn of oil, and anointed him in the midst of his brethren: and the Spirit of the LORD came upon David from that day forward. So Samuel rose up, and went to Ramah.

He is the author of change

Zechariah 4:6: Then he answered and spake unto me, saying, This is the word of the LORD unto Zerubbabel, saying, Not by might, nor by power, but by my spirit, saith the LORD of hosts.

He was the beginning/life/creation

Genesis 1:2: And the earth was without form, and void; and darkness was upon the face of the deep. And the Spirit of God moved upon the face of the waters.

Job 33:4: The Spirit of God hath made me, and the breath of the Almighty hath given me life.

Psalms 104:30: Thou sendest forth thy spirit, they are created: and thou renewest the face of the earth.

He is counsel

Isaiah 11:2: And the spirit of the LORD shall rest upon him, the spirit of wisdom and understanding, the spirit of counsel and might, the spirit of knowledge and of the fear of the LORD;

He is deliverance

Judges 3:10: And the Spirit of the LORD came upon him, and he judged Israel, and went out to war: and the LORD delivered Chushan-rish-athaim king of Mesopotamia into his hand; and his hand prevailed against Chushan-rishathaim.

Judges 11:29: Then the Spirit of the LORD came upon Jephthah, and he passed over Gilead, and Manasseh, and passed over Mizpeh of Gil-ead, and from Mizpeh of Gilead he passed over unto the children of Ammon.

He is direction/guidance

1 Kings 18:12: And it shall come to pass, as soon as I am gone from thee, that the Spirit of the LORD shall carry thee whither I know not; and so when I come and tell Ahab, and he cannot find thee, he shall slay me: but I thy servant fear the LORD from my youth.

He commissions

Isaiah 48:16: Come ye near unto me, hear ye this; I have not spoken in secret from the beginning; from the time that it was, there am I: and now the Lord GOD, and his Spirit, hath sent me.

He is excellence

Daniel 5:12: Forasmuch as an excellent spirit, and knowledge, and understanding, interpreting of dreams, and shewing of hard sentences, and dissolving of doubts, were found in the same Daniel, whom the king named Belteshazzar: now let Daniel be called, and he will shew the interpretation.

Daniel 6:3: Then this Daniel was preferred above the presidents and princes, because an excellent spirit was in him; and the king thought to set him over the whole realm.

He garnishes the Heavens

Job 26:13: By his spirit he hath garnished the heavens; his hand hath formed the crooked serpent formed the crooked serpent.

He is grace

Zechariah 12:10: And I will pour upon the house of David, and upon the inhabitants of Jerusalem, the spirit of grace and of supplications: and they shall look upon me whom they have pierced, and they shall mourn for him, as one mourneth for his only son, and shall be in bitterness for him, as one that is in bitterness for his firstborn.

He instructs

Nehemiah 9:20: Thou gavest also thy good spirit to instruct them, and withheldest not thy manna from their mouth, and gavest them water for their thirst.

He is knowledge

Exodus 31:3: And I have filled him with the spirit of God, in wisdom, and in understanding, and in knowledge, and in all manner of workmanship,

Exodus 35:31: And he hath filled him with the spirit of God, in wisdom, in understanding, and in knowledge, and in all manner of workmanship;

Isaiah 11:2: And the spirit of the LORD shall rest upon him, the spirit of wisdom and understanding, the spirit of counsel and might, the spirit of knowledge and of the fear of the LORD;

He leads to the Glory of God (inner court)

Ezekiel 43:5: So the spirit took me up, and brought me into the inner court; and, behold, the glory of the LORD filled the house.

He gives life

Ezekiel 37:14: And shall put my spirit in you, and ye shall live, and I shall place you in your own land: then shall ye know that I the LORD have spoken it, and performed it, saith the LORD. (valley of dry bones)

He is Mighty

Isaiah 11:2: And the spirit of the LORD shall rest upon him, the spirit of wisdom and understanding, the spirit of counsel and might, the spirit of knowledge and of the fear of the LORD;

He overpowers the enemy

1 Samuel 19:20: And Saul sent messengers to take David: and when they saw the company of the prophets prophesying, and Samuel standing as appointed over them, the Spirit of God was upon the messengers of Saul, and they also prophesied.

1 Samuel 19:21: And when it was told Saul, he sent other messengers, and they prophesied likewise. And Saul sent messengers again the third time, and they prophesied also.

1 Samuel 19:22: Then went he also to Ramah, and came to a great well that *is* in Sechu: and he asked and said, Where *are* Samuel and David? And *one* said, Behold, *they be* at Naioth in Ramah.

1 Samuel 19:23: And he went thither to Naioth in Ramah: and the Spirit of God was upon him also, and he went on, and prophesied, until he came to Naioth in Ramah.

He gives power

Micah 3:8: But truly I am full of power by the spirit of the LORD, and of judgment, and of might, to declare unto Jacob his transgression, and to Israel his sin.

He allows us to preach/bind the brokenhearted/ proclaim liberty/open prisons

Isaiah 61:1: The Spirit of the Lord GOD is upon me; because the LORD hath anointed me to preach good tidings unto the meek; he hath sent me to bind up the brokenhearted, to proclaim liberty to the captives, and the opening of the prison to them that are bound;

He prepares vessels for great tasks (favor)

Joshua

Numbers 27:18: And the LORD said unto Moses, Take thee Joshua the son of Nun, a man in whom is the spirit, and lay thine hand upon him;

Deuteronomy 34:9: And Joshua the son of Nun was full of the spirit of wisdom; for Moses had laid his hands upon him: and the children of Israel hearkened unto him, and did as the LORD commanded Moses.

Gideon

Judges 6:34: But the Spirit of the LORD came upon Gideon, and he blew a trumpet; and Abi-ezer was gathered after him.

He prepares others to help bear burdens (help fight or bring in the troops)

Numbers 11:17: And I will come down and talk with thee there: and I will take of the spirit which is upon thee, and will put it upon them; and they shall bear the burden of the people with thee, that thou bear it not thyself alone.

Numbers 11:25: And the LORD came down in a cloud, and spake unto him, and took of the spirit that was upon him, and gave it unto the seventy elders: and it came to pass, that, when the spirit rested upon them, they prophesied, and did not cease.

He enables the flow of the prophetic

Numbers 11:25: And the LORD came down in a cloud, and spake unto him, and took of the spirit that was upon him, and gave it unto the seventy elders: and it came to pass, that, when the spirit rested upon them, they prophesied, and did not cease.

Numbers 11:26: But there remained two of the men in the camp, the name of the one was Eldad, and the name of the other Medad: and the spirit rested upon them; and they were of them that were written, but went not out unto the tabernacle: and they prophesied in the camp.

Numbers 11:29: And Moses said unto him, Enviest thou for my sake? would God that all the LORD's people were prophets, and that the LORD would put his spirit upon them!

Numbers 24:2: And Balaam lifted up his eyes, and he saw Israel abiding in his tents according to their tribes; and the spirit of God came upon him. (See also chaps 22 and 24)

1 Samuel 10:6: And the Spirit of the LORD will come upon thee, and thou shalt prophesy with them, and shalt be turned into another man.

1 Samuel 10:10: And when they came thither to the hill, behold, a company of prophets met him; and the Spirit of God came upon him, and he prophesied among them.

1 Samuel 19:20: And Saul sent messengers to take David: and when they saw the company of the prophets prophesying, and Samuel standing as appointed over them, the Spirit of God was upon the messengers of Saul, and they also prophesied.

1 Samuel 19:21: And when it was told Saul, he sent other messengers, and they prophesied likewise. And Saul sent messengers again the third time, and they prophesied also.

1 Samuel 19:22: Then went he also to Ramah, and came to a great well that *is* in Sechu: and he asked and said, Where *are* Samuel and David? And *one* said, Behold, *they be* at Naioth in Ramah.

1 Samuel 19:23: And he went thither to Naioth in Ramah: and the Spirit of God was upon him also, and he went on, and prophesied, until he came to Naioth in Ramah.

Nehemiah 9:30: Yet many years didst thou forbear them, and testifiedst against them by thy spirit in thy prophets: yet would they not give ear: therefore gavest thou them into the hand of the people of the lands.

Joel 2:28: And it shall come to pass afterward, that I will pour out my spirit upon all flesh; and your sons and your daughters shall prophesy, your old men shall dream dreams, your young men shall see visions:

Joel 2:29: And also upon the servants and upon the handmaids in those days will I pour out my spirit.

Micah 2:6: Prophesy ye not, say they to them that prophesy: they shall not prophesy to them, that they shall not take shame.

Micah 2:7: O thou that art named the house of Jacob, is the spirit of the LORD straitened? are these his doings? do not my words do good to him that walketh uprightly?

Zechariah 7:12: Yea, they made their hearts as an adamant stone, lest they should hear the law, and the words which the LORD of hosts hath sent in his spirit by the former prophets: therefore came a great wrath from the LORD of hosts.

Challenging prophetic word from the Lord

2 Chronicles 15:1: And the Spirit of God came upon Azariah the son of Oded:

2 Chronicles 15:2: And he went out to meet Asa, and said unto him, Hear ye me, Asa, and all Judah and Benjamin; The LORD is with you, while ye be with him; and if ye seek him, he will be found of you; but if ye forsake him, he will forsake you.

2 Chronicles 24:20: And the Spirit of God came upon Zechariah the son of Jehoiada the priest, which stood above the people, and said unto them, Thus saith God, Why transgress ye the commandments of the LORD, that ye cannot prosper? because ye have forsaken the LORD, he hath also forsaken you.

Encouraging prophetic word from the Lord

2 Chronicles 20:14: Then upon Jahaziel the son of Zechariah, the son of Benaiah, the son of Jeiel, the son of Mattaniah, a Levite of the sons of Asaph, came the Spirit of the LORD in the midst of the congregation;

2 Chronicles 20:15: And he said, Hearken ye, all Judah, and ye inhabitants of Jerusalem, and thou king Jehoshaphat, Thus saith the LORD unto you, Be not afraid nor dismayed by reason of this great multitude; for the battle is not yours, but God's.

2 Chronicles 20:16: Tomorrow go ye down against them: behold, they come up by the cliff of Ziz; and ye shall find them at the end of the brook, before the wilderness of Jeruel.

He uses vessels to prophesy/dream/have visions

Joel 2:28: And it shall come to pass afterward, that I will pour out my spirit upon all flesh; and your sons and your daughters shall prophesy, your old men shall dream dreams, your young men shall see visions:

Joel 2:29: And also upon the servants and upon the handmaids in those days will I pour out my spirit.

He protects from the enemy

1 Samuel 19:20: And Saul sent messengers to take David: and when they saw the company of the prophets prophesying, and Samuel standing as appointed over them, the Spirit of God was upon the messengers of Saul, and they also prophesied.

1 Samuel 19:21: And when it was told Saul, he sent other messengers, and they prophesied likewise. And Saul sent messengers again the third time, and they prophesied also.

1 Samuel:19:23: And he went thither to Naioth in Ramah: and the Spirit of God was upon him also, and he went on, and prophesied, until he came to Naioth in Ramah.

Haggai 2:5: According to the word that I covenanted with you when ye came out of Egypt, so my spirit remaineth among you: fear ye not.

Isaiah 59:19: So shall they fear the name of the LORD from the west, and his glory from the rising of the sun. When the enemy shall come in like a flood, the Spirit of the LORD shall lift up a standard against him.

He recruits others

1 Samuel 19:20: And Saul sent messengers to take David: and when they saw the company of the prophets prophesying, and Samuel standing as appointed over them, the Spirit of God was upon the messengers of Saul, and they also prophesied.

1 Samuel 19:21: And when it was told Saul, he sent other messengers, and they prophesied likewise. And Saul sent messengers again the third time, and they prophesied also.

1 Samuel 19:22: Then went he also to Ramah, and came to a great well that *is* in Sechu: and he asked and said, Where *are* Samuel and David? And *one* said, Behold, *they be* at Naioth in Ramah.

1 Samuel 19:23: And he went thither to Naioth in Ramah: and the Spirit of God was upon him also, and he went on, and prophesied, until he came to Naioth in Ramah.

He gives revelation/interpretation

Joseph and his interpretations (Genesis 41)

Genesis 41:38: And Pharaoh said unto his servants, Can we find such a one as this is, a man in whom the Spirit of God is?

Daniel 4:18: This dream I king Nebuchadnezzar have seen. Now thou, O Belteshazzar, declare the interpretation thereof, forasmuch as all the wise men of my kingdom are not able to make known unto me the interpretation: but thou art able; for the spirit of the holy gods is in thee.

He gives reverence

(Demands it)

2 Kings 2:15: And when the sons of the prophets which were to view at Jericho saw him, they said, The spirit of Elijah doth rest on Elisha. And they came to meet him, and bowed themselves to the ground before him.

1 Samuel 19:20: And Saul sent messengers to take David: and when they saw the company of the prophets prophesying, and Samuel standing as appointed over them, the Spirit of God was upon the messengers of Saul, and they also prophesied.

(Helps to release it – fear of the Lord)

Isaiah 11:2: And the spirit of the LORD shall rest upon him, the spirit of wisdom and understanding, the spirit of counsel and might, the spirit of knowledge and of the fear of the LORD;

He gives rest

Isaiah 63:14: As a beast goeth down into the valley, the Spirit of the LORD caused him to rest: so didst thou lead thy people, to make thyself a glorious name.

He allows us to see the face of God

Ezekiel 39:29: Neither will I hide my face any more from them: for I have poured out my spirit upon the house of Israel, saith the Lord GOD.

He sends you

Isaiah 48:16: Come ye near unto me, hear ye this; I have not spoken in secret from the beginning; from the time that it was, there am I: and now the Lord GOD, and his Spirit, hath sent me.

He speaks to you and instructs you

Ezekiel 11:5: And the Spirit of the LORD fell upon me, and said unto me, Speak; Thus saith the LORD; Thus have ye said, O house of Israel: for I know the things that come into your mind, every one of them.

His departure (yielding from/loss of pretection)

1 Samuel 16:14: But the Spirit of the LORD departed from Saul, and an evil spirit from the LORD troubled him.

1 Samuel 16:15: And Saul's servants said unto him, Behold now, an evil spirit from God troubleth thee.

1 Samuel 16:16: Let our lord now command thy servants, which are before thee, to seek out a man, who is a cunning player on an harp: and it shall come to pass, when the evil spirit from God is upon thee, that he shall play with his hand, and thou shalt be well.

See also I Samuel 18:10-30 and I Samuel 19:9-24.

He is strength

Judges 14:6: And the Spirit of the LORD came mightily upon him, and he rent him as he would have rent a kid, and he had nothing in his hand: but he told not his father or his mother what he had done.

Judges 14:19: And the Spirit of the LORD came upon him, and he went down to Ashkelon, and slew thirty men of them, and took their spoil, and gave change of garments unto them which expounded the riddle. And his anger was kindled, and he went up to his father's house.

He anoints

Moses → Joshua

Deuteronomy 34:9: And Joshua the son of Nun was full of the spirit of wisdom; for Moses had laid his hands upon him: and the children of Israel hearkened unto him, and did as the LORD commanded Moses.

Saul → David

1 Samuel 16:13: Then Samuel took the horn of oil, and anointed him in the midst of his brethren: and the Spirit of the LORD came upon David from that day forward. So Samuel rose up, and went to Ramah.

Elijah → Elisha

2 Kings 2:9: And it came to pass, when they were gone over, that Elijah said unto Elisha, Ask what I shall do for thee, before I be taken away from thee. And Elisha said, I pray thee, let a double portion of thy spirit be upon me.

He is the Spirit of supplications (asking for something earnestly or humbly)

Zechariah 12:10: And I will pour upon the house of David, and upon the inhabitants of Jerusalem, the spirit of grace and of supplications: and they shall look upon me whom they have pierced, and they shall mourn for him, as one mourneth for his only son, and shall be in bitterness for him, as one that is in bitterness for his firstborn.

He helps us understand

Exodus 31:3: And I have filled him with the spirit of God, in wisdom, and in understanding, and in knowledge, and in all manner of workmanship,

Exodus 35:31: And he hath filled him with the spirit of God, in wisdom, in understanding, and in knowledge, and in all manner of workmanship;

Daniel 5:11: There is a man in thy kingdom, in whom is the spirit of the holy gods; and in the days of thy father light and understanding and wisdom, like the wisdom of the gods, was found in him; whom the king Nebuchadnezzar thy father, the king, I say, thy father, made master of the magicians, astrologers, Chaldeans, and soothsayers;

Daniel 5:14: I have even heard of thee, that the spirit of the gods is in thee, and that light and understanding and excellent wisdom is found in thee.

Isaiah 11:2: And the spirit of the LORD shall rest upon him, the spirit of wisdom and understanding, the spirit of counsel and might, the spirit of knowledge and of the fear of the LORD;

He gives us victory

Judges 3:10: And the Spirit of the LORD came upon him, and he judged Israel, and went out to war: and the LORD delivered Chushan-rishathaim king of Mesopotamia into his hand; and his hand prevailed against Chushan-rishathaim.

Judges 15:14: And when he came unto Lehi, the Philistines shouted against him: and the Spirit of the LORD came mightily upon him, and the cords that were upon his arms became as flax that was burnt with fire, and his bands loosed from off his hands.

Judges 15:15: And he found a new jawbone of an ass, and put forth his hand, and took it, and slew a thousand men therewith.

He gives us visions

Ezekiel 11:24: Afterwards the spirit took me up, and brought me in a vision by the Spirit of God into Chaldea, to them of the captivity. So the vision that I had seen went up from me.

Ezekiel 37:1: The hand of the LORD was upon me, and carried me out in the spirit of the LORD, and set me down in the midst of the valley which *was* full of bones,

Joel 2:28: And it shall come to pass afterward, that I will pour out my spirit upon all flesh; and your sons and your daughters shall prophesy, your old men shall dream dreams, your young men shall see visions:

Joel 2:29: And also upon the servants and upon the handmaids in those days will I pour out my spirit.

He helps us walk in God's statutes/keep God's judgments

Ezekiel 36:27: And I will put my spirit within you, and cause you to walk in my statutes, and ye shall keep my judgments, and do them.

He gives us wisdom

Exodus 28:3: And thou shalt speak unto all that are wise hearted, whom I have filled with the spirit of wisdom, that they may make Aaron's garments to consecrate him, that he may minister unto me in the priest's office.

Exodus 31:3: And I have filled him with the spirit of God, in wisdom, and in understanding, and in knowledge, and in all manner of workmanship,

Exodus 35:31: And he hath filled him with the spirit of God, in wisdom, in understanding, and in knowledge, and in all manner of workmanship;

Deuteronomy 34:9: And Joshua the son of Nun was full of the spirit of wisdom; for Moses had laid his hands upon him: and the children of Israel hearkened unto him, and did as the LORD commanded Moses. (Note that Moses laid his hand upon Joshua)

Daniel 5:11: There is a man in thy kingdom, in whom is the spirit of the holy gods; and in the days of thy father light and understanding and wisdom, like the wisdom of the gods, was found in him; whom the king Nebuchadnezzar thy father, the king, I say, thy father, made master of the magicians, astrologers, Chaldeans, and soothsayers;

Daniel 5:14: I have even heard of thee, that the spirit of the gods is in thee, and that light and understanding and excellent wisdom is found in thee.

Isaiah 11:2: And the spirit of the LORD shall rest upon him, the spirit of wisdom and understanding, the spirit of counsel and might, the spirit of knowledge and of the fear of the LORD;

IV.

The Holy Spirit in the New Testament

5

The Holy Spirit in the New Testament (Letter)

Dear Holy Spirit:

I am excited, because this is where the fun begins. As a new Christian, I will honestly say that I did not know who You were. Your name and Your work were often mentioned either as part of a story or as a casual mention. You were the great Unknown, and so many of us avoided conversations that had anything to do with You.

As I studied, I realized how little I knew and how much more I needed to know about You. When John spoke of being baptized by fire (Matthew 3:11 and Luke 3:16), and Jesus promised us a guide (John 16:13-15), I wanted to know You as a guide, and I want to know what that means. Holy Spirit, I, like so many other, had (and still have) so many questions. I found many answers throughout this study.

I want the reader to discover what I discovered. I want the reader to know more about the Spirit that Jesus promised (John 7:38,39, Acts 1:4-8.) I want to highlight the story of how You introduced Yourself to the Church by pouring Yourself on 120 people in the upper room (Acts 2:1-4). An outpouring so mighty that it drew people who were open to hearing about Jesus. I wanted to show the reader how You gave Yourself to the House of Cornelius (Acts 10) and fed their

faith and their hunger. I wanted to show them a Spirit who empowered Stephen in strength to do such great works that the religious leaders could not deny the God in Him. (Acts 6:8-Acts 7: 60).

I genuinely want every reader to discover You in ways that I have. My prayer is that every reader will take a moment or two and answer the following questions as they find out more about you. Find my personal answer to question 4 in the manifestation section of this book.

1. Holy Spirit, who are You and are You for me?
2. How do You work, and how can You work through me?
3. What do I need to do or be to allow You to work in me?
4. Do you only work through church leaders?
5. Holy Spirit, what are You capable of, and how can You help me become a better Christian?
6. How can You help me fight the devil and his army?
7. Why did Jesus really send You to us?

I hope that every answer reaffirms why we need You in our lives and our Christian walk. I hope that every answer leads us to discover who You are and who You want to be to us. I learned so much about You during this portion of the study, and I pray that whoever reads the following will learn more about who You are.

I feel that You were just as excited as I was to take this journey. You know that lives are being touched around me the more I know and the more I give through You. I encourage every reader to find that excitement and discover who you truly are through a place of hunger.

Thank You Holy Spirit for being You. I love You and I cherish every day I can serve You.

Love,
Your servant,
Marco

6

The Holy Spirit in the New Testament (Scriptures)

He abides with us forever

John 14:16: And I will pray the Father, and he shall give you another Comforter, that he may abide with you forever;

He enables us to abound (overflow) in Hope

Romans 15:13: Now the God of hope fill you with all joy and peace in believing, that ye may abound in hope, through the power of the Holy Ghost.

He gives us access to the Father

Ephesians 2:18: For through him we both have access by one Spirit unto the Father.

He encourages our acknowledgement of God (from believer)

1 John 4:2: Hereby know ye the Spirit of God: Every spirit that confesseth that Jesus Christ is come in the flesh is of God:

1 John 4:13: Hereby know we that we dwell in him, and he in us, because he hath given us of his Spirit.

He adopts us

Romans 8:15: For ye have not received the spirit of bondage again to fear; but ye have received the Spirit of adoption, whereby we cry, Abba, Father.

Galatians 4:6: And because ye are sons, God hath sent forth the Spirit of his Son into your hearts, crying, Abba, Father.

He is the anointing

(See Unction – G5545 – Thayer's)

1 John 2:27: But the anointing which ye have received of him abideth in you, and ye need not that any man teach you: but as the same anointing teacheth you of all things, and is truth, and is no lie, and even as it hath taught you, ye shall abide in him.

He encourages our appointment (requirement)/ selection

Ministration

Acts 6:3: Wherefore, brethren, look ye out among you seven men of honest report, full of the Holy Ghost and wisdom, whom we may appoint over this business.

Elders/Overseers

Acts 20:28: Take heed therefore unto yourselves, and to all the flock, over the which the Holy Ghost hath made you overseers, to feed the church of God, which he hath purchased with his own blood.

Minister of God

2 Corinthians 6:4: But in all things approving ourselves as the ministers of God…

2 Corinthians 6:6:…. by the Holy Ghost…

He baptizes us

John 1:33: And I knew him not: but he that sent me to baptize with water, the same said unto me, Upon whom thou shalt see the Spirit descending, and remaining on him, the same is he which baptizeth with the Holy Ghost.

John 3:6: That which is born of the flesh is flesh; and that which is born of the Spirit is spirit.

Matthew 3:11: I indeed baptize you with water unto repentance: but he that cometh after me is mightier than I, whose shoes I am not worthy to bear: he shall baptize you with the Holy Ghost, and with fire:

Matthew 28:19: Go ye therefore, and teach all nations, baptizing them in the name of the Father, and of the Son, and of the Holy Ghost:

Matthew 1:8: I indeed have baptized you with water: but he shall baptize you with the Holy Ghost.

1 Corinthians 12:13: For by one Spirit are we all baptized into one body, whether we be Jews or Gentiles, whether we be bond or free; and have been all made to drink into one Spirit.

He bears witness or record

Beareth (G3140) – to prove or confirm by testimony, through the baptism and death of Christ and the Holy Spirit giving souls assurance of this expiation. (I John 5:6-9)

Romans 8:16: The Spirit itself beareth witness with our spirit, that we are the children of God:

1 John 5:6: This is he that came by water and blood, even Jesus Christ; not by water only, but by water and blood. And it is the Spirit that beareth witness, because the Spirit is truth.

1 John 5:7: For there are three that bear record in heaven, the Father, the Word, and the Holy Ghost: and these three are one.

1 John 5:8: And there are three that bear witness in earth, the Spirit, and the water, and the blood: and these three agree in one.

1 John 5:9: If we receive the witness of men, the witness of God is greater: for this is the witness of God which he hath testified of his Son.

He helps us become an example

1 Timothy 4:12: Let no man despise thy youth; but be thou an example of the believers, in word, in conversation, in charity, in spirit, in faith, in purity.

He helps cast out devils

Matthew 12:28: But if I cast out devils by the Spirit of God, then the kingdom of God is come unto you.

He helps us change into the image of God

2 Corinthians 3:18: But we all, with open face beholding as in a glass the glory of the Lord, are changed into the same image from glory to glory, even as by the Spirit of the Lord.

He is our Comforter

John 14:16: And I will pray the Father, and he shall give you another Comforter, that he may abide with you forever;

John 14:26: But the Comforter, which is the Holy Ghost, whom the Father will send in my name, he shall teach you all things, and bring all things to your remembrance, whatsoever I have said unto you.

John 15:26: But when the Comforter is come, whom I will send unto you from the Father, even the Spirit of truth, which proceedeth from the Father, he shall testify of me:

John 16:7: Nevertheless I tell you the truth; It is expedient for you that I go away: for if I go not away, the Comforter will not come unto you; but if I depart, I will send him unto you.

Acts 9:31: Then had the churches rest throughout all Judaea and Galilee and Samaria, and were edified; and walking in the fear of the Lord, and in the comfort of the Holy Ghost, were multiplied.

He brings communion

2 Corinthians 13:14: The grace of the Lord Jesus Christ, and the love of God, and the communion of the Holy Ghost, be with you all. Amen.

He declares the Son of God with power

Romans 1:4: And declared to be the Son of God with power, according to the spirit of holiness, by the resurrection from the dead:

He delivers the Gospel

1 Thessalonians 1:5: For our gospel came not unto you in word only, but also in power, and in the Holy Ghost, and in much assurance; as ye know what manner of men we were among you for your sake.

He gives us discernment/perception

Mark 2:8: And immediately when Jesus perceived in his spirit that they so reasoned within themselves, he said unto them, Why reason ye these things in your hearts?

John 13:21: When Jesus had thus said, he was troubled in spirit, and testified, and said, Verily, verily, I say unto you, that one of you shall betray me.

1 Corinthians 12:10: … to another discerning of spirits….

He is the divider and giver of spiritual gifts

1 Corinthians 12:4: Now there are diversities of gifts, but the same Spirit.

1 Corinthians 12:11: But all these worketh that one and the selfsame Spirit, dividing to every man severally as he will.

(Gifts - G5486 - charisma)

1 Corinthians 1:7: So that ye come behind in no gift; waiting for the coming of our Lord Jesus Christ:

1 Corinthians 12:31: But covet earnestly the best gifts: and yet shew I unto you a more excellent way.

1 Peter 4:10: As every man hath received the gift, even so minister the same one to another, as good stewards of the manifold grace of God.

He draws in the multitudes

All of Acts 2 and Acts 6

Acts 2:38: Then Peter said unto them, Repent, and be baptized every one of you in the name of Jesus Christ for the remission of sins, and ye shall receive the gift of the Holy Ghost.

Acts 2:41: Then they that gladly received his word were baptized: and the same day there were added unto them about three thousand souls.

He gives dreams

Acts 2:17: And it shall come to pass in the last days, saith God, I will pour out of my Spirit upon all flesh: and your sons and your daughters shall prophesy, and your young men shall see visions, and your old men shall dream dreams:

He is our earnest (pledge)

(Earnest - G728 - Pledge)

2 Corinthians 1:22: Who hath also sealed us, and given the earnest of the Spirit in our hearts.

2 Corinthians 5:5: Now he that hath wrought us for the selfsame thing is God, who also hath given unto us the earnest of the Spirit.

He edifies the church

1 Corinthians 14:12: Even so ye, forasmuch as ye are zealous of spiritual gifts, seek that ye may excel to the edifying of the church.

He is eternal

Hebrews 9:14: How much more shall the blood of Christ, who through the eternal Spirit offered himself without spot to God, purge your conscience from dead works to serve the living God?

He delivers everlasting life/entrance into the Kingdom of Heaven

John 3:5: Jesus answered, Verily, verily, I say unto thee, Except a man be born of water and of the Spirit, he cannot enter into the kingdom of God.

Romans 8:9: But ye are not in the flesh, but in the Spirit, if so be that the Spirit of God dwell in you. Now if any man have not the Spirit of Christ, he is none of his.

Galatians 6:8: For he that soweth to his flesh shall of the flesh reap corruption; but he that soweth to the Spirit shall of the Spirit reap life everlasting.

Soweth (G4687) – to do those things which satisfy the nature and promptings of.

He is our faith

2 Corinthians 4:13: We having the same spirit of faith, according as it is written, I believed, and therefore have I spoken; we also believe, and therefore speak;

1 Corinthians 12:9: To another faith by the same Spirit; to another the gifts of healing by the same Spirit;

He fellowships

Philippians 2:1: If there be therefore any consolation in Christ, if any comfort of love, if any fellowship of the Spirit, if any bowels and mercies,

He fills us (as God's gift to us)

Acts 2:4: And they were all filled with the Holy Ghost, and began to speak with other tongues, as the Spirit gave them utterance.

Ephesians 5:18 And be not drunk with wine, wherein is excess; but be filled with the Spirit;

He fills us for purpose (acknowledges God's purpose)

Luke 1:15: For he shall be great in the sight of the Lord, and shall drink neither wine nor strong drink; and he shall be filled with the Holy Ghost, even from his mother's womb.

Luke 1:41: And it came to pass, that, when Elisabeth heard the salutation of Mary, the babe leaped in her womb; and Elisabeth was filled with the Holy Ghost:

Luke 1:67: And his father Zacharias was filled with the Holy Ghost, and prophesied, saying,

Acts 1:3: To whom also he shewed himself alive after his passion by many infallible proofs, being seen of them forty days, and speaking of the things pertaining to the kingdom of God:

Acts 1:4: And, being assembled together with *them,* commanded them that they should not depart from Jerusalem, but wait for the promise of the Father, which, *saith he,* ye have heard of me.

Acts 1:5: For John truly baptized with water; but ye shall be baptized with the Holy Ghost not many days hence.

Acts 2:1: And when the day of Pentecost was fully come, they were all with one accord in one place.

Acts 2:2: And suddenly there came a sound from heaven as of a rushing mighty wind, and it filled all the house where they were sitting.

Acts 2:3: And there appeared unto them cloven tongues like as of fire, and it sat upon each of them.

Acts 2:4: And they were all filled with the Holy Ghost, and began to speak with other tongues, as the Spirit gave them utterance.

He gives us first fruits

Romans 8:23: And not only they, but ourselves also, which have the firstfruits of the Spirit, even we ourselves groan within ourselves, waiting for the adoption, to wit, the redemption of our body.

He forbids/suffers not (give permission)

Acts 16:6: Now when they had gone throughout Phrygia and the region of Galatia, and were forbidden of the Holy Ghost to preach the word in Asia,

Acts 16:7: After they were come to Mysia, they assayed to go into Bithynia: but the Spirit suffered them not.

He is freedom/liberty

Luke 4:18: The Spirit of the Lord is upon me, because he hath anointed me to preach the gospel to the poor; he hath sent me to heal the broken-hearted, to preach deliverance to the captives, and recovering of sight to the blind, to set at liberty them that are bruised,

2 Corinthians 3:17: Now the Lord is that Spirit: and where the Spirit of the Lord is, there is liberty.

Romans 8:2: For the law of the Spirit of life in Christ Jesus hath made me free from the law of sin and death.

Galatians 5:18: But if ye be led of the Spirit, ye are not under the law.

He is freedom from condemnation

Romans 8:1: There is therefore now no condemnation to them which are in Christ Jesus, who walk not after the flesh, but after the Spirit.

He is His fruit

- Love
- Joy
- Peace
- Longsuffering
- Gentleness
- Goodness
- Faith
- Meekness
- Temperance
- ***He is in all*** goodness, righteousness and truth

Galatians 5:22: But the fruit of the Spirit is love, joy, peace, longsuffering, gentleness, goodness, faith,

Galatians 5:23: Meekness, temperance: against such there is no law.

1 Corinthians 12:9: To another faith by the same Spirit;

Ephesians 5:9: (For the fruit of the Spirit is in all goodness and righteousness and truth;)

Ephesians 5:10: Proving what is acceptable unto the Lord.

He fulfills righteousness of the law

Romans 8:4: That the righteousness of the law might be fulfilled in us, who walk not after the flesh, but after the Spirit.

He is a precious gift (from Jesus/God)

Luke 11:13: If ye then, being evil, know how to give good gifts unto your children: how much more shall your heavenly Father give the Holy Spirit to them that ask him?

John 1:33: And I knew him not: but he that sent me to baptize with water, the same said unto me, Upon whom thou shalt see the Spirit descending, and remaining on him, the same is he which baptizeth with the Holy Ghost.

John 7:38: He that believeth on me, as the scripture hath said, out of his belly shall flow rivers of living water.

John 7:39: (But this spake he of the Spirit, which they that believe on him should receive: for the Holy Ghost was not yet given; because that Jesus was not yet glorified.

John 16:7: Nevertheless I tell you the truth; It is expedient for you that I go away: for if I go not away, the Comforter will not come unto you; but if I depart, I will send him unto you.

John 20:22: And when he had said this, he breathed on them, and saith unto them, Receive ye the Holy Ghost:

Acts 5:32: And we are his witnesses of these things; and so is also the Holy Ghost, whom God hath given to them that obey him.

Romans 5:5: And hope maketh not ashamed; because the love of God is shed abroad in our hearts by the Holy Ghost which is given unto us.

1 Thessalonians 4:8: He therefore that despiseth, despiseth not man, but God, who hath also given unto us his holy Spirit.

1 John 4:13: Hereby know we that we dwell in him, and he in us, because he hath given us of his Spirit.

He is a gift from God/Jesus for our salvation

Matthew 1:18: Now the birth of Jesus Christ was on this wise: When as his mother Mary was espoused to Joseph, before they came together, she was found with child of the Holy Ghost.

Matthew 1:20: But while he thought on these things, behold, the angel of the Lord appeared unto him in a dream, saying, Joseph, thou son of David, fear not to take unto thee Mary thy wife: for that which is conceived in her is of the Holy Ghost.

Luke 1:35: And the angel answered and said unto her, The Holy Ghost shall come upon thee, and the power of the Highest shall overshadow thee: therefore also that holy thing which shall be born of thee shall be called the Son of God.

Hebrews 9:14: How much more shall the blood of Christ, who through the eternal Spirit offered himself without spot to God, purge your conscience from dead works to serve the living God?

He is a gift in you

(Gift – G5486- charisma)

1 Timothy 4:14: Neglect not the gift that is in thee, which was given thee by prophecy, with the laying on of the hands of the presbytery.

He gives commandments from Jesus/God

Acts 1:2: Until the day in which he was taken up, after that he through the Holy Ghost had given commandments unto the apostles whom he had chosen:

He is grace

Hebrews 10:29: Of how much sorer punishment, suppose ye, shall he be thought worthy, who hath trodden under foot the Son of God, and hath counted the blood of the covenant, wherewith he was sanctified, an unholy thing, and hath done despite unto the Spirit of grace?

He guides us

John 16:13: Howbeit when he, the Spirit of truth, is come, he will guide you into all truth: for he shall not speak of himself; but whatsoever he shall hear, that shall he speak: and he will shew you things to come.

Galatians 5:25: If we live in the Spirit, let us also walk in the Spirit.

He coordinates the habitation of God (or place where God dwells)

(see Temple of the Holy Ghost)

Ephesians 2:22: In whom ye also are builded together for an habitation of God through the Spirit.

He uses us to heal broken hearts

Luke 4:18: The Spirit of the Lord is upon me, because he hath anointed me to preach the gospel to the poor; he hath sent me to heal the brokenhearted, to preach deliverance to the captives, and recovering of sight to the blind, to set at liberty them that are bruised,

He allows us to hear the voice of God

Revelation 1:10: I was in the Spirit on the Lord's day, and heard behind me a great voice, as of a trumpet,

He helps with our infirmities

Romans 8:26: Likewise the Spirit also helpeth our infirmities: for we know not what we should pray for as we ought: but the Spirit itself maketh intercession for us with groanings which cannot be uttered.

He inspires us

Mark 12:36: For David himself said by the Holy Ghost, The LORD said to my Lord, Sit thou on my right hand, till I make thine enemies thy footstool.

He instructs us

Acts 8:29: Then the Spirit said unto Philip, Go near, and join thyself to this chariot.

Acts 8:39: And when they were come up out of the water, the Spirit of the Lord caught away Philip, that the eunuch saw him no more: and he went on his way rejoicing.

Acts 11:12: And the Spirit bade me go with them, nothing doubting. Moreover these six brethren accompanied me, and we entered into the man's house:

He intercedes/groans on our behalf

Romans 8:26: Likewise the Spirit also helpeth our infirmities: for we know not what we should pray for as we ought: but the Spirit itself maketh intercession for us with groanings which cannot be uttered.

Romans 8:27: And he that searcheth the hearts knoweth what is the mind of the Spirit, because he maketh intercession for the saints according to the will of God.

He is joy

Romans 14:17: For the kingdom of God is not meat and drink; but righteousness, and peace, and joy in the Holy Ghost.

Galatians 5:22: But the fruit of the Spirit is love, joy, peace, longsuffering, gentleness, goodness, faith,

1 Thessalonians 1:6: And ye became followers of us, and of the Lord, having received the word in much affliction, with joy of the Holy Ghost:

He justifies/confirms/acknowledges

Matthew 3:16: And Jesus, when he was baptized, went up straightway out of the water: and, lo, the heavens were opened unto him, and he saw the Spirit of God descending like a dove, and lighting upon him:

Mark 1:10: And straightway coming up out of the water, he saw the heavens opened, and the Spirit like a dove descending upon him:

John 1:32: And John bare record, saying, I saw the Spirit descending from heaven like a dove, and it abode upon him.

John 1:33: And I knew him not: but he that sent me to baptize with water, the same said unto me, Upon whom thou shalt see the Spirit descending, and remaining on him, the same is he which baptizeth with the Holy Ghost.

1 Timothy 3:16: And without controversy great is the mystery of godliness: God was manifest in the flesh, justified in the Spirit, seen of angels, preached unto the Gentiles, believed on in the world, received up into glory.

He leads (Direction)

(**Led**, Romans 8:14, **(G71)** – to move of forces and influences affecting the mind)

Matthew 4:1: Then was Jesus led up of the Spirit into the wilderness to be tempted of the devil.

Mark 1:12: And immediately the Spirit driveth him into the wilderness.

Luke 2:27: And he came by the Spirit into the temple: and when the parents brought in the child Jesus, to do for him after the custom of the law,

Luke 4:1: And Jesus being full of the Holy Ghost returned from Jordan, and was led by the Spirit into the wilderness,

Acts 8:39: And when they were come up out of the water, the Spirit of the Lord caught away Philip, that the eunuch saw him no more: and he went on his way rejoicing.

Acts 15:28: For it seemed good to the Holy Ghost, and to us, to lay upon you no greater burden than these necessary things;

John 3:8: The wind bloweth where it listeth, and thou hearest the sound thereof, but canst not tell whence it cometh, and whither it goeth: so is every one that is born of the Spirit.

Romans 8:14: For as many as are led by the Spirit of God, they are the sons of God.

Galatians 5:18: But if ye be led of the Spirit, ye are not under the law.

He is life

Romans 8:10: And if Christ be in you, the body is dead because of sin; but the Spirit is life because of righteousness.

Romans 8:11: But if the Spirit of him that raised up Jesus from the dead dwell in you, he that raised up Christ from the dead shall also quicken your mortal bodies by his Spirit that dwelleth in you.

Romans 8:13: For if ye live after the flesh, ye shall die: but if ye through the Spirit do mortify the deeds of the body, ye shall live.

2 Corinthians 3:6: Who also hath made us able ministers of the new testament; not of the letter, but of the spirit: for the letter killeth, but the spirit giveth **life**. See G2227.

1 Peter 4:6: For for this cause was the gospel preached also to them that are dead, that they might be judged according to men in the flesh, but live according to God in the spirit.

1 John 3:24: And he that keepeth his commandments dwelleth in him, and he in him. And hereby we know that he abideth in us, by the Spirit which he hath given us.

Revelations 11:11: And after three days and an half the Spirit of life from God entered into them, and they stood upon their feet; and great fear fell upon them which saw them.

He is love

Romans 15:30: Now I beseech you, brethren, for the Lord Jesus Christ's sake, and for the love of the Spirit, that ye strive together with me in your prayers to God for me;

Galatians 5:22: But the fruit of the Spirit is love, joy, peace, longsuffering, gentleness, goodness, faith,

Colossians 1:8: Who also declared unto us your love in the Spirit.

2 Timothy 1:7: For God hath not given us the spirit of fear; but of power, and of love, and of a sound mind.

His manifestation is for every man to profit

1 Corinthians 12:7: But the manifestation of the Spirit is given to every man to profit withal.

He stirs maturity

1 Corinthians 3:1: And I, brethren, could not speak unto you as unto spiritual, but as unto carnal, even as unto babes in Christ.

His mind requires searching hearts to know it

Romans 8:27: And he that searcheth the hearts knoweth what is the mind of the Spirit, because he maketh intercession for the saints according to the will of God.

He needs us to mind things of Him

Romans 8:5: For they that are after the flesh do mind the things of the flesh; but they that are after the Spirit the things of the Spirit.

He should be in our ministry

Galatians 3:5: He therefore that ministereth to you the Spirit, and worketh miracles among you, doeth he it by the works of the law, or by the hearing of faith?

He should be in our worship

John 4:23: But the hour cometh, and now is, when the true worshippers shall worship the Father in spirit and in truth: for the Father seeketh such to worship him.

John 4:24: God is a Spirit: and they that worship him must worship him in spirit and in truth.

Philippians 3:3: For we are the circumcision, which worship God in the spirit, and rejoice in Christ Jesus, and have no confidence in the flesh.

If He leads, we are not under the law

Galatians 5:18: But if ye be led of the Spirit, ye are not under the law.

He helps us obey the truth

1 Peter 1:22: Seeing ye have purified your souls in obeying the truth through the Spirit unto unfeigned love of the brethren, see that ye love one another with a pure heart fervently:

He is part of the Christian

1 Corinthians 7:40: But she is happier if she so abide, after my judgment: and I think also that I have the Spirit of God.

He is peace

Romans 14:17: For the kingdom of God is not meat and drink; but righteousness, and peace, and joy in the Holy Ghost.

Galatians 5:22: But the fruit of the Spirit is love, joy, peace, longsuffering, gentleness, goodness, faith,

He is power (signs and wonders)

Luke 4:14: And Jesus returned in the power of the Spirit into Galilee: and there went out a fame of him through all the region round about.

Acts 6:8: And Stephen, full of faith and power, did great wonders and miracles among the people.

Acts 7:55: But he (*Stephen*), being full of the Holy Ghost, looked up stedfastly into heaven, and saw the glory of God, and Jesus standing on the right hand of God,

Romans 15:19: Through mighty signs and wonders, by the power of the Spirit of God; so that from Jerusalem, and round about unto Illyricum, I have fully preached the gospel of Christ.

2 Timothy 1:7: For God hath not given us the spirit of fear; but of power, and of love, and of a sound mind.

He helps us pray

(Supplication G1162- of prayers imploring God's aid in some particular matter)

Ephesians 6:18: Praying always with all prayer and supplication in the Spirit, and watching thereunto with all perseverance and supplication for all saints;

Jude 1:20: But ye, beloved, building up yourselves on your most holy faith, praying in the Holy Ghost,

He leads us to preach the gospel/deliverance/ sight recovery

Luke 4:18: The Spirit of the Lord is upon me, because he hath anointed me to preach the gospel to the poor; he hath sent me to heal the brokenhearted, to preach deliverance to the captives, and recovering of sight to the blind, to set at liberty them that are bruised,

1 Peter 1:12: Unto whom it was revealed, that not unto themselves, but unto us they did minister the things, which are now reported unto you by them that have preached the gospel unto you with the Holy Ghost sent down from heaven; which things the angels desire to look into.

He is Prophecy

Luke 1:67: And his father Zacharias was filled with the Holy Ghost, and prophesied…

John 16:13: Howbeit when he, the Spirit of truth, is come, he will guide you into all truth: for he shall not speak of himself; but whatsoever he shall hear, that shall he speak: and he will shew you things to come.

Acts 2:17: And it shall come to pass in the last days, saith God, I will pour out of my Spirit upon all flesh: and your sons and your daughters shall prophesy, and your young men shall see visions, and your old men shall dream dreams:

Acts 2:18: And on my servants and on my handmaidens I will pour out in those days of my Spirit; and they shall prophesy:

Acts 11:28: And there stood up one of them named Agabus, and signified by the Spirit that there should be great dearth throughout all the world: which came to pass in the days of Claudius Caesar.

Acts 21:4: And finding disciples, we tarried there seven days: who said to Paul through the Spirit, that he should not go up to Jerusalem.

Acts 21:10: And as we tarried there many days, there came down from Judaea a certain prophet, named Agabus.

Acts 21:11: And when he was come unto us, he took Paul's girdle, and bound his own hands and feet, and said, Thus saith the Holy Ghost, So shall the Jews at Jerusalem bind the man that owneth this girdle, and shall deliver him into the hands of the Gentiles.

He protects from lust (when we follow His lead)

Galatians 5:16: This I say then, Walk in the Spirit, and ye shall not fulfil the lust of the flesh.

Galatians 5:17: For the flesh lusteth against the Spirit, and the Spirit against the flesh: and these are contrary the one to the other: so that ye cannot do the things that ye would.

He purifies our soul

1 Peter 1:22: Seeing ye have purified your souls in obeying the truth through the Spirit unto unfeigned love of the brethren, see that ye love one another with a pure heart fervently:

He quickens and gives life

Quickeneth/Quickened -(G2227) – to give (John 6:63), quickened as respects the Spirit endued with and greater powers of life (I Peter 3:18)

John 6:63: It is the spirit that quickeneth; the flesh profiteth nothing: the words that I speak unto you, they are spirit, and they are life.

Romans 8:11: But if the Spirit of him that raised up Jesus from the dead dwell in you, he that raised up Christ from the dead shall also quicken your mortal bodies by his Spirit that dwelleth in you.

2 Corinthians 3:6: Who also hath made us able ministers of the new testament; not of the letter, but of the spirit: for the letter killeth, but the spirit giveth **life**. (by spiritual power to arouse and invigorate)

1 Peter 3:18: For Christ also hath once suffered for sins, the just for the unjust, that he might bring us to God, being put to death in the flesh, but quickened by the Spirit:

With Him, you will receive persecution

Galatians 4:29: But as then he that was born after the flesh persecuted him that was born after the Spirit, even so it is now.

With Him, you will receive reproach

1 Peter 4:14: If ye be reproached for the name of Christ, happy are ye; for the spirit of glory and of God resteth upon you: on their part he is evil spoken of, but on your part he is glorified.

He helps the blind recover sight

Luke 4:18: The Spirit of the Lord is upon me, because he hath anointed me to preach the gospel to the poor; he hath sent me to heal the broken-hearted, to preach deliverance to the captives, and recovering of sight to the blind, to set at liberty them that are bruised,

He renews you

Titus 3:5: Not by works of righteousness which we have done, but according to his mercy he saved us, by the washing of regeneration, and renewing of the Holy Ghost;

He reproves the world of sin, righteousness and of judgment

Reprove (1651) - to convict, refute, confute

John 16:7: Nevertheless I tell you the truth; It is expedient for you that I go away: for if I go not away, the Comforter will not come unto you; but if I depart, I will send him unto you.

John 16:8: And when he is come, he will reprove the world of sin, and of righteousness, and of judgment:

John 16:9: Of sin, because they believe not on me;

John 16:10: Of righteousness, because I go to my Father, and ye see me no more;

John 16:11: Of judgment, because the prince of this world is judged.

He reveals things to us

Luke 2:26: And it was revealed unto him by the Holy Ghost, that he should not see death, before he had seen the Lord's Christ.

John 16:13: Howbeit when he, the Spirit of truth, is come, he will guide you into all truth: for he shall not speak of himself; but whatsoever he shall hear, that shall he speak: and he will shew you things to come.

Acts 10:19: While Peter thought on the vision, the Spirit said unto him, Behold, three men seek thee.

Ephesians 1:17: That the God of our Lord Jesus Christ, the Father of glory, may give unto you the spirit of wisdom and revelation in the knowledge of him:

Ephesians 3:5: Which in other ages was not made known unto the sons of men, as it is now revealed unto his holy apostles and prophets by the Spirit;

From God

John 16:13: Howbeit when he, the Spirit of truth, is come, he will guide you into all truth: for he shall not speak of himself; but whatsoever he shall hear, that shall he speak: and he will shew you things to come.

1 Corinthians 2:10: But God hath revealed them unto us by his Spirit: for the Spirit searcheth all things, yea, the deep things of God.

1 Corinthians 2:11: For what man knoweth the things of a man, save the spirit of man which is in him? even so the things of God knoweth no man, but the Spirit of God.

He gives us reverence/respect from those around us

Acts 6:10: And they were not able to resist the wisdom and the spirit by which he spake.

Revelations 11:11: And after three days and an half the Spirit of life from God entered into them, and they stood upon their feet; and great fear fell upon them which saw them.

He is righteousness/peace/joy

Romans 14:17: For the kingdom of God is not meat and drink; but righteousness, and peace, and joy in the Holy Ghost.

He sanctifies us (purification)

Romans 15:16: That I should be the minister of Jesus Christ to the Gentiles, ministering the gospel of God, that the offering up of the Gentiles might be acceptable, being sanctified by the Holy Ghost.

2 Thessalonians 2:13: But we are bound to give thanks alway to God for you, brethren beloved of the Lord, because God hath from the beginning chosen you to salvation through sanctification of the Spirit and belief of the truth:

1 Peter 1:2: Elect according to the foreknowledge of God the Father, through sanctification of the Spirit, unto obedience and sprinkling of the blood of Jesus Christ: Grace unto you, and peace, be multiplied.

He seals us unto Christ, redemption

Ephesians 1:13: In whom ye also trusted, after that ye heard the word of truth, the gospel of your salvation: in whom also after that ye believed, ye were sealed with that holy Spirit of promise,

Ephesians 4:30: And grieve not the holy Spirit of God, whereby ye are sealed unto the day of redemption.

He gives us a sound mind

2 Timothy 1:7: For God hath not given us the spirit of fear; but of power, and of love, and of a sound mind.

He separates and sends us forth for ministry

Acts 13:2: As they ministered to the Lord, and fasted, the Holy Ghost said, Separate me Barnabas and Saul for the work whereunto I have called them.

Acts 13:4: So they, being sent forth by the Holy Ghost, departed unto Seleucia; and from thence they sailed to Cyprus.

He sheds God's loves in our hearts

Romans 5:5: And hope maketh not ashamed; because the love of God is shed abroad in our hearts by the Holy Ghost which is given unto us.

He shows judgement

Matthew 12:18: Behold my servant, whom I have chosen; my beloved, in whom my soul is well pleased: I will put my spirit upon him, and he shall shew judgment to the Gentiles.

He gives us speech and preaching

Matthew 10:20: For it is not ye that speak, but the Spirit of your Father which speaketh in you.

Mark 13:11: But when they shall lead you, and deliver you up, take no thought beforehand what ye shall speak, neither do ye premeditate: but whatsoever shall be given you in that hour, that speak ye: for it is not ye that speak, but the Holy Ghost.

Luke 12:12: For the Holy Ghost shall teach you in the same hour what ye ought to say.

1 Corinthians 2:4: And my speech and my preaching was not with enticing words of man's wisdom, but in demonstration of the Spirit and of power:

Hebrews 3:7: Wherefore (as the Holy Ghost saith, To day if ye will hear his voice,

1 Timothy 4:1: Now the Spirit speaketh expressly, that in the latter times some shall depart from the faith, giving heed to seducing spirits, and doctrines of devils;

2 Peter 1:21: For the prophecy came not in old time by the will of man: but holy men of God spake as they were moved by the Holy Ghost.

He gives speech in other tongues

Acts 2:4: And they were all filled with the Holy Ghost, and began to speak with other tongues, as the Spirit gave them utterance.

1 Corinthians 12:10: To another the working of miracles; to another prophecy; to another discerning of spirits; to another *divers* kinds of tongues; to another the interpretation of tongues:

His spiritual gifts

(1 Corinthians 14:1:... and desire spiritual gifts)

1. Wisdom

1 Corinthians 12:8: For to one is given by the Spirit the word of wisdom; to another the word of knowledge by the same Spirit;

2. Word of Knowledge

1 Corinthians 12:8: For to one is given by the Spirit the word of wisdom; to another the word of knowledge by the same Spirit;

3. Faith

1 Corinthians 12:9: To another faith by the same Spirit; to another the gifts of healing by the same Spirit;

4. Healing

1 Corinthians 12:9: To another faith by the same Spirit; to another the gifts of healing by the same Spirit;

5. Miracles

1 Corinthians 12:10: To another the working of miracles; to another prophecy; to another discerning of spirits; to another divers kinds of tongues; to another the interpretation of tongues:

6. Prophecy

1 Corinthians 12:10: To another the working of miracles; to another prophecy; to another discerning of spirits; to another divers kinds of tongues; to another the interpretation of tongues:

7. Discerning of Spirits

1 Corinthians 12:10: To another the working of miracles; to another prophecy; to another discerning of spirits; to another divers kinds of tongues; to another the interpretation of tongues:

8. Divers kinds of tongues

1 Corinthians 12:10: To another the working of miracles; to another prophecy; to another discerning of spirits; to another divers kinds of tongues; to another the interpretation of tongues:

9. Interpretation of tongues

1 Corinthians 12:10: To another the working of miracles; to another prophecy; to another discerning of spirits; to another divers kinds of tongues; to another the interpretation of tongues:

He is strength

Luke 1:80: And the child grew, and waxed strong in spirit, and was in the deserts till the day of his shewing unto Israel.

Luke 2:40: And the child grew, and waxed strong in spirit, filled with wisdom: and the grace of God was upon him.

He strengthens with might

Ephesians 3:16: That he would grant you, according to the riches of his glory, to be strengthened with might by his Spirit in the inner man;

He is our supplier

Philippians 1:19: For I know that this shall turn to my salvation through your prayer, and the supply of the Spirit of Jesus Christ,

He is the Sword (Word of God)

Ephesians 6:17: And take the helmet of salvation, and the sword of the Spirit, which is the word of God:

He gives us a taste of the heavenly gift

Hebrews 6:4: For it is impossible for those who were once enlightened, and have tasted of the heavenly gift, and were made partakers of the Holy Ghost,

He teaches/brings things to our remembrance

John 14:26: But the Comforter, which is the Holy Ghost, whom the Father will send in my name, he shall teach you all things, and bring all things to your remembrance, whatsoever I have said unto you.

Luke 12:12: For the Holy Ghost shall teach you in the same hour what ye ought to say.

He teaches knowledge and wisdom

1 Corinthians 2:12: Now we have received, not the spirit of the world, but the spirit which is of God; that we might know the things that are freely given to us of God.

1 Corinthians 2:13: Which things also we speak, not in the words which man's wisdom teacheth, but which the Holy Ghost teacheth; comparing spiritual things with spiritual.

He should be the Tenant of our temple

1 Corinthians 3:16: Know ye not that ye are the temple of God, and that the Spirit of God dwelleth in you?

1 Corinthians 6:19: What? know ye not that your body is the temple of the Holy Ghost which is in you, which ye have of God, and ye are not your own?

2 Timothy 1:14: That good thing which was committed unto thee keep by the Holy Ghost which dwelleth in us.

He testifies about Jesus

John 15:26: But when the Comforter is come, whom I will send unto you from the Father, even the Spirit of truth, which proceedeth from the Father, he shall testify of me:

1 Peter 1:11: Searching what, or what manner of time the Spirit of Christ which was in them did signify, when it testified beforehand the sufferings of Christ, and the glory that should follow.

He testifies that Jesus is the Son of God

Mark 1:10: And straightway coming up out of the water, he saw the heavens opened, and the Spirit like a dove descending upon him:

Luke 3:22: And the Holy Ghost descended in a bodily shape like a dove upon him, and a voice came from heaven, which said, Thou art my beloved Son; in thee I am well pleased.

Romans 1:4: And declared to be the Son of God with power, according to the spirit of holiness, by the resurrection from the dead:

Revelation 19:10: And I fell at his feet to worship him. And he said unto me, See thou do it not: I am thy fellowservant, and of thy brethren that have the testimony of Jesus: worship God: for the testimony of Jesus is the spirit of prophecy.

He is truth

John 14:17: Even the Spirit of truth; whom the world cannot receive, because it seeth him not, neither knoweth him: but ye know him; for he dwelleth with you, and shall be in you.

John 15:26: But when the Comforter is come, whom I will send unto you from the Father, even the Spirit of truth, which proceedeth from the Father, he shall testify of me:

John 16:13: Howbeit when he, the Spirit of truth, is come, he will guide you into all truth: for he shall not speak of himself; but whatsoever he shall hear, that shall he speak: and he will shew you things to come.

1 John 5:6: This is he that came by water and blood, even Jesus Christ; not by water only, but by water and blood. And it is the Spirit that beareth witness, because the Spirit is truth.

He gives us an unction

(see anointing - G5545) (Thayer's)

1 John 2:20: But ye have an unction from the Holy One, and ye know all things.

He brings unity

Ephesians 4:3: Endeavouring to keep the unity of the Spirit in the bond of peace.

He gives a unknown tongue from God so that we can speak to God

1 Corinthians 14:2: For he that speaketh in an unknown tongue speaketh not unto men, but unto God: for no man understandeth him; howbeit in the spirit he speaketh mysteries.

1 Corinthians 14:14: For if I pray in an unknown tongue, my spirit prayeth, but my understanding is unfruitful.

1 Corinthians 14:15: What is it then? I will pray with the spirit, and I will pray with the understanding also: I will sing with the spirit, and I will sing with the understanding also.

He helps us pray

(**Supplication -(G1162)**- of prayers imploring God's aid in some particular matter) (Thayer's)

Ephesians 6:18: Praying always with all prayer and supplication in the Spirit, and watching thereunto with all perseverance and supplication for all saints;

Jude 1:20: But ye, beloved, building up yourselves on your most holy faith, praying in the Holy Ghost,

He gives visions

Acts 2:17: And it shall come to pass in the last days, saith God, I will pour out of my Spirit upon all flesh: and your sons and your daughters shall prophesy, and your young men shall see visions, and your old men shall dream dreams:

He uses our voice

Matthew 10:20: For it is not ye that speak, but the Spirit of your Father which speaketh in you.

In Him, we wait for hope of righteousness

Galatians 5:5: For we through the Spirit wait for the hope of righteousness by faith.

He washes, sanctifies, and justifies us

1 Corinthians 6:11: And such were some of you: but ye are washed, but ye are sanctified, but ye are justified in the name of the Lord Jesus, and by the Spirit of our God.

His weapons of warfare.

(Ephesians 6:10-17)

Ephesians 6:10: Finally, my brethren, be strong in the Lord, and in the power of his might.

Ephesians 6:11: Put on the whole armour of God, that ye may be able to stand against the wiles of the devil.

Ephesians 6:12: For we wrestle not against flesh and blood, but against principalities, against powers, against the rulers of the darkness of this world, against spiritual wickedness in high *places.*

Ephesians 6:13: Wherefore take unto you the whole armour of God, that ye may be able to withstand in the evil day, and having done all, to stand.

Ephesians 6:14: Stand therefore, having your loins girt about with truth, and having on the breastplate of righteousness;

Ephesians 6:15: And your feet shod with the preparation of the gospel of peace;

Ephesians 6:16: Above all, taking the shield of faith, wherewith ye shall be able to quench all the fiery darts of the wicked.

Ephesians 6:17: And take the helmet of salvation, and the sword of the Spirit, which is the word of God:

His (our) armor

Belt of Truth

1 John 5:6: This is he that came by water and blood, even Jesus Christ; not by water only, but by water and blood. And it is the Spirit that beareth witness, because the Spirit is truth.

Breastplate of Righteousness

Romans 14:17: For the kingdom of God is not meat and drink; but righteousness, and peace, and joy in the Holy Ghost.

Sandals of Peace

Romans 14:17: For the kingdom of God is not meat and drink; but righteousness, and peace, and joy in the Holy Ghost.

Galatians 5:22: But the fruit of the Spirit is love, joy, peace, longsuffering, gentleness, goodness, faith,

Shield of Faith

Galatians 5:22: But the fruit of the Spirit is love, joy, peace, longsuffering, gentleness, goodness, faith,

1 Corinthians 12:9: To another faith by the same Spirit; to another the gifts of healing by the same Spirit;

Helmet of Salvation

2 Thessalonians 2:13: But we are bound to give thanks alway to God for you, brethren beloved of the Lord, because God hath from the beginning chosen you to salvation through sanctification of the Spirit and belief of the truth:

Ephesians 1:13: In whom ye also trusted, after that ye heard the word of truth, the gospel of your salvation: in whom also after that ye believed, ye were sealed with that holy Spirit of promise,

Sword of the Spirit

Ephesians 6:17: And take the helmet of salvation, and the sword of the Spirit, which is the word of God:

He is willing/ready against the flesh

Matthew 26:41: Watch and pray, that ye enter not into temptation: the spirit indeed is willing, but the flesh is weak.

Mark 14:38: Watch ye and pray, lest ye enter into temptation. The spirit truly is ready, but the flesh is weak.

He witnesses (as a witness or helps us to do so)

Acts 20:23: Save that the Holy Ghost witnesseth in every city, saying that bonds and afflictions abide me.

Romans 9:1: I say the truth in Christ, I lie not, my conscience also bearing me witness in the Holy Ghost,

Hebrews 2:4: God also bearing them witness, both with signs and wonders, and with divers miracles, and gifts of the Holy Ghost, according to his own will?

Hebrews 10:15: Whereof the Holy Ghost also is a witness to us: for after that he had said before,

He speaks the word(s) of God

John 3:34: For he whom God hath sent speaketh the words of God: for God giveth not the Spirit by measure unto him.

John 6:63: It is the spirit that quickeneth; the flesh profiteth nothing: the words that I speak unto you, they are spirit, and they are life.

Ephesians 6:17: And take the helmet of salvation, and the sword of the Spirit, which is the word of God:

Revelations 2:7: He that hath an ear, let him hear what the Spirit saith unto the churches; To him that overcometh will I give to eat of the tree of life, which is in the midst of the paradise of God.

Revelations 2:11: He that hath an ear, let him hear what the Spirit saith unto the churches; He that overcometh shall not be hurt of the second death.

Revelations 2:17: He that hath an ear, let him hear what the Spirit saith unto the churches; To him that overcometh will I give to eat of the hidden manna, and will give him a white stone, and in the stone a new name written, which no man knoweth saving he that receiveth it.

Revelations 2:29: He that hath an ear, let him hear what the Spirit saith unto the churches.

Revelations 3:6: He that hath an ear, let him hear what the Spirit saith unto the churches.

Revelations 3:13: He that hath an ear, let him hear what the Spirit saith unto the churches.

Revelations 3:22: He that hath an ear, let him hear what the Spirit saith unto the churches.

Revelations 14:13: And I heard a voice from heaven saying unto me, Write, Blessed are the dead which die in the Lord from henceforth: Yea, saith the Spirit, that they may rest from their labours; and their works do follow them.

Revelations 22:17: And the Spirit and the bride say, Come. And let him that heareth say, Come. And let him that is athirst come. And whosoever will, let him take the water of life freely.

He should be in our worship

John 4:23: But the hour cometh, and now is, when the true worshippers shall worship the Father in spirit and in truth: for the Father seeketh such to worship him.

John 4:24: God is a Spirit: and they that worship him must worship him in spirit and in truth.

Philippians 3:3: For we are the circumcision, which worship God in the spirit, and rejoice in Christ Jesus, and have no confidence in the flesh.

He helps us become an epistle of Christ

2 Corinthians 3:3: Forasmuch as ye are manifestly declared to be the epistle of Christ ministered by us, written not with ink, but with the Spirit of the living God; not in tables of stone, but in fleshy tables of the heart.

V.

WARNING! DO NOT DO THE FOLLOWING TO THE HOLY SPIRIT (OR BE WITHOUT HIM)

7

WARNING! DO NOT DO THE FOLLOWING TO HOLY SPIRIT (OR BE WITHOUT HIM) (Letter)

Dear Holy Spirit:

I want to thank you so much for being patient with me. You know, when I first heard about you, I did not know what to think about You. I knew nothing about who You were, what You wanted to be to me. I had no opinion on You because when I was younger, I never had a Bible study that taught me everything You were. As a result, when I first heard about You, it was too early to have a thought or an opinion of You as I knew so little. I needed this study.

From this study, I learned two things. First, I learned more about who You were and what You desired to be in and through me and second, I also discovered what I should **not** do. As I first read the following and integrated it with other information that I learned, I realized that in You, there is something gentle, honest and so precious that the following Scriptures speak to protect You and Your presence in our lives.

I took it as a stern reminder to be gentle and honest with You in every way. I should be so connected with You that I immediately know when I might do something that hurts You or hurts someone who You want me to minister to. I promise that I will work extremely hard to not do the following and I ask that You guide and speak to me so that I will always be aware of this. I love You and I never want to hurt You.

Love,
Your servant,
Marco

8

WARNING! DO NOT DO THE FOLLOWING TO HOLY SPIRIT (OR BE WITHOUT HIM) (Scriptures)

Do not ignore Spiritual Gifts

1 Corinthians 12:1: Now concerning spiritual gifts, brethren, I would not have you ignorant.

1 Corinthians 12:3: Wherefore I give you to understand, that no man speaking by the Spirit of God calleth Jesus accursed: and that no man can say that Jesus is the Lord, but by the Holy Ghost.

Do not begin in the Spirit and be made perfect by the flesh

Galatians 3:3: Are ye so foolish? having begun in the Spirit, are ye now made perfect by the flesh?

Do not blaspheme the Holy Spirit

Blasphemy (G988) – railing, reviling, speech injurious to another's good name (Thayer's)

Blaspheme (G987) – of those who by contemptuous speech intentionally come short of the reverence due to God or sacred things (also rail at or revile) (Thayer's)

Matthew 12:31: Wherefore I say unto you, All manner of sin and blasphemy shall be forgiven unto men: but the blasphemy against the Holy Ghost shall not be forgiven unto men.

Matthew 12:32: And whosoever speaketh a word against the Son of man, it shall be forgiven him: but whosoever speaketh against the Holy Ghost, it shall not be forgiven him, neither in this world, neither in the world to come.

Mark 3:29: But he that shall blaspheme against the Holy Ghost hath never forgiveness, but is in danger of eternal damnation:

Luke 12:10: And whosoever shall speak a word against the Son of man, it shall be forgiven him: but unto him that blasphemeth against the Holy Ghost it shall not be forgiven.

Do not grieve the Holy Spirit

Grieve (G3076) – grieve or offend

Ephesians 4:30: And grieve not the holy Spirit of God, whereby ye are sealed unto the day of redemption.

Do not resist the Holy Spirit

Acts 7:51: Ye stiffnecked and uncircumcised in heart and ears, ye do always resist the Holy Ghost: as your fathers did, so do ye.

Do not resist those who are filled with the Holy Spirit

(Gamailel and Peter)

Acts 5:38: And now I say unto you, Refrain from these men, and let them alone: for if this counsel or this work be of men, it will come to nought:

Acts 5:39: But if it be of God, ye cannot overthrow it; lest haply ye be found even to fight against God.

(Pharisees and Paul)

Acts 23:9: And there arose a great cry: and the scribes that were of the Pharisees' part arose, and strove, saying, We find no evil in this man: but if a spirit or an angel hath spoken to him, let us not fight against God.

Do not quench the Holy Spirit

Quench (G4570) – extinguish, quench, suppress divine influence (Thayer's)

1 Thessalonians 5:19: Quench not the Spirit

Do not separate yourself from the Holy Spirit

Sensual (5591) – governed by the sensual nature (Thayer's)

Jude 1:19: These be they who separate themselves, sensual, having not the Spirit.

Do not speak against the Holy Spirit

Matthew 12:32: And whosoever speaketh a word against the Son of man, it shall be forgiven him: but whosoever speaketh against the Holy Ghost, it shall not be forgiven him, neither in this world, neither in the world to come.

Do not tempt or lie to the Holy Spirit

2 Chronicles 18:23: Then Zedekiah the son of Chenaanah came near, and smote Micaiah upon the cheek, and said, Which way went the Spirit of the LORD from me to speak unto thee?

2 Chronicles 18:24: And Micaiah said, Behold, thou shalt see on that day when thou shalt go into an inner chamber to hide thyself.

Lie (G5574) – to speak deliberate falsehoods (Thayer's)

Tempt (G3985) – **test** (Thayer's)
(Annaias and Sapphira)

Acts 5:1: But a certain man named Ananias, with Sapphira his wife, sold a possession,

Acts 5:2: And kept back part of the price, his wife also being privy to it, and brought a certain part, and laid it at the apostles' feet.

Acts 5:3: But Peter said, Ananias, why hath Satan filled thine heart to lie to the Holy Ghost, and to keep back part of the price of the land?

Acts 5:4: Whiles it remained, was it not thine own? and after it was sold, was it not in thine own power? why hast thou conceived this thing in thine heart? thou hast not lied unto men, but unto God.

Acts 5:5: And Ananias hearing these words fell down, and gave up the ghost: and great fear came on all them that heard these things.

Acts 5:6: And the young men arose, wound him up, and carried him out, and buried him.

Acts 5:7: And it was about the space of three hours after, when his wife, not knowing what was done, came in.

Acts 5:8: And Peter answered unto her, Tell me whether ye sold the land for so much? And she said, Yea, for so much.

Acts 5:9: Then Peter said unto her, How is it that ye have agreed together to tempt the Spirit of the Lord? behold, the feet of them which have buried thy husband are at the door, and shall carry thee out.

Acts 5:10: Then fell she down straightway at his feet, and yielded up the ghost: and the young men came in, and found her dead, and, carrying her forth, buried her by her husband.

Do not try to cast out devils without the Spirit of God

Acts 19:14: And there were seven sons of one Sceva, a Jew, and chief of the priests, which did so.

Acts 19:15: And the evil spirit answered and said, Jesus I know, and Paul I know; but who are ye?

Acts 19:16: And the man in whom the evil spirit was leaped on them, and overcame them, and prevailed against them, so that they fled out of that house naked and wounded.

Do not use the natural mind to understand the Holy Spirit and receive not

1 Corinthians 2:14: But the natural man receiveth not the things of the Spirit of God: for they are foolishness unto him: neither can he know them, because they are spiritually discerned.

Do not vex the Holy Spirit

Vex- (6087) worry, pain, make hurt, grieve, cause distress to

Isaiah 63:10: But they rebelled, and vexed his holy Spirit: therefore he was turned to be their enemy, and he fought against them.

Do not lose the Holy Spirit's protection

(no longer sealed – Ephesians 4:30) = loss of protection

King Saul

1 Samuel 16:14: But the Spirit of the LORD departed from Saul, and an evil spirit from the LORD troubled him.

1 Samuel 16:15: And Saul's servants said unto him, Behold now, an evil spirit from God troubleth thee.

1 Samuel 16:16: Let our lord now command thy servants, which are before thee, to seek out a man, who is a cunning player on an harp: and it shall come to pass, when the evil spirit from God is upon thee, that he shall play with his hand, and thou shalt be well.

VI.

Vessels used by the Holy Spirit

9

Vessels used by the Holy Spirit (Letter)

Dear Friend in Christ:

I want the following to encourage you. The Holy Spirit wants to fill you. He wants to walk with you. He wants to work with you. In Romans 8 we read the following:

Romans 8:14: For as many as are led by the Spirit of God, they are the sons of God.

Romans 8:19: For the earnest expectation of the creature waiteth for the manifestation of the sons of God.

The world is waiting for us to be completely led by the Spirit. This section is a special section because it shows that anyone can be a vessel for the Spirit. All too often, we place a Spirit-led walk at the feet of church leadership when we need to pick up a torch and walk in that promise (Acts 2:39). We need to embrace the fire (Matthew 3:11, Luke 3:16) we have been baptized in (or want to be baptized in) and let that fire show us what needs to burn and what needs to be refined.

God can use anyone He wants, and He promised His Spirit to all of us. For me, I have to remind myself to yield on a daily basis and that is not easy. I am human. I have the frailties of a human like the men we read about. There are times when I doubted God's presence and reality just like Thomas. There are times that my faith wavers like Peter.

When I have these challenges, I remind myself that I am a vessel that the Spirit resides in – a vessel that can and will because God can and will.

This part of the book, although brief, inspires me. It reminds me that I don't have to preach a certain way or at all. I don't have to sing a certain way or play an instrument. I don't have to have a title of any kind or be licensed in any way. I just simply need a filling of His Spirit and be ready to serve when He needs me to serve. I am just an ordinary guy who loves God and loves working through His Spirit.

Ever since I began this journey many years ago, I always gravitated to a passage that has now grown on me. I call it my "mission scripture". That scripture is Isaiah 61:1 and it says the following:

Isaiah 61:1 The Spirit of the Lord GOD *is* upon me; because the LORD hath anointed me to preach good tidings unto the meek; he hath sent me to bind up the brokenhearted, to proclaim liberty to the captives, and the opening of the prison to *them that are* bound;

There are select portions of this passage that seem to be recurring themes in my walk. The Lord sent me so many who needed help healing their broken hearts and also help them to proclaim liberty to the internal prisons that held them captive. Every mission requires the Spirit and His guidance.

I always give people the example of someone trying to break into prison. In the movies, we see the prisoner with a spoon who slowly chisels through cinderblock with that spoon for years or finds a way to hide in laundry. When the Spirit guides me to break into a prison, there are many things to consider.

For example, is that person ready for freedom? This may sound like a question with an obvious answer, but there are times when many are not ready especially in places where the pain is incredibly deep.

I could go on and on, but I want to stress that the Holy Spirit needs all of us because no one is omnipresent. We need Him, and He needs us every time for anyone.

Your friend in Christ,
Marco

10

Vessels used by the Holy Spirit (Scriptures)

God the Father, Son and Holy Spirit are One

1 John 5:7: For there are three that bear record in heaven, the Father, the Word, and the Holy Ghost: and these three are one.

1 John 5:8: And there are three that bear witness in earth, the Spirit, and the water, and the blood: and these three agree in one.

Now the vessels and their gifts/opportunities

His vessels in the Old Testament

Moses (Levite)

(Isaiah 63:11) – used Moses to deliver the people

Isaiah 63:11: Then he remembered the days of old, Moses, and his people, saying, Where is he that brought them up out of the sea with the shepherd of his flock? where is he that put his holy Spirit within him?

Seventy Elders

(Numbers 11:25) – Prophesied

Numbers 11:25: And the LORD came down in a cloud, and spake unto him, and took of the spirit that was upon him, and gave it unto the seventy elders: and it came to pass, that, when the spirit rested upon them, they prophesied, and did not cease.

Eldad

(Numbers 11:26) – Prophecy

Numbers 11:26: But there remained two of the men in the camp, the name of the one was Eldad, and the name of the other Medad: and the spirit rested upon them; and they were of them that were written, but went not out unto the tabernacle: and they prophesied in the camp.

Medad

(Numbers 11:26)- Prophecy

Numbers 11:26: But there remained two of the men in the camp, the name of the one was Eldad, and the name of the other Medad: and the spirit rested upon them; and they were of them that were written, but went not out unto the tabernacle: and they prophesied in the camp.

Joseph

(Genesis 41) – Revelation of Dreams (word of knowledge)

Genesis 41:38: And Pharaoh said unto his servants, Can we find such a one as this is, a man in whom the Spirit of God is?

Genesis 41:39: And Pharaoh said unto Joseph, Forasmuch as God hath shewed thee all this, there is none so discreet and wise as thou art:

Baalam

(Numbers 24) – Prophecy

Numbers 24:2: And Balaam lifted up his eyes, and he saw Israel abiding in his tents according to their tribes; and the spirit of God came upon him.

Joshua

(Deuteronomy 34:9, Numbers 27:18) – entered the Promised Land and took down Jericho

Deuteronomy 34:9: And Joshua the son of Nun was full of the spirit of wisdom; for Moses had laid his hands upon him: and the children of Israel hearkened unto him, and did as the LORD commanded Moses.

Numbers 27:18: And the LORD said unto Moses, Take thee Joshua the son of Nun, a man in whom is the spirit, and lay thine hand upon him;

Othiniel

(Judges 3:9, 10) – Prevailed in war

Judges 3:9: And when the children of Israel cried unto the LORD, the LORD raised up a deliverer to the children of Israel, who delivered them, even Othniel the son of Kenaz, Caleb's younger brother.

Judges 3:10: And the Spirit of the LORD came upon him, and he judged Israel, and went out to war: and the LORD delivered Chushan-rishathaim king of Mesopotamia into his hand; and his hand prevailed against Chushanrishathaim.

Gideon

(Judges 6:34) – Prevailed in war

Judges 6:34: But the Spirit of the LORD came upon Gideon, and he blew a trumpet; and Abiezer was gathered after him.

Jepthah

(Judges 11:29) – Prevailed in war

Judges 11:29: Then the Spirit of the LORD came upon Jephthah, and he passed over Gilead, and Manasseh, and passed over Mizpeh of Gilead, and from Mizpeh of Gilead he passed over unto the children of Ammon.

Samson

(Judges 13:24, 25) – Source of his strength

Judges 13:24: And the woman bare a son, and called his name Samson: and the child grew, and the LORD blessed him.

Judges 13:25: And the Spirit of the LORD began to move him at times in the camp of Dan between Zorah and Eshtaol.

Saul

(1 Samuel 10:6, 10, 11:6) – King of Israel

1 Samuel 10:6: And the Spirit of the LORD will come upon thee, and thou shalt prophesy with them, and shalt be turned into another man.

1 Samuel 10:10: And when they came thither to the hill, behold, a company of prophets met him; and the Spirit of God came upon him, and he prophesied among them.

1 Samuel 11:6: And the Spirit of God came upon Saul when he heard those tidings, and his anger was kindled greatly.

Saul in error (1 Samuel 16:14-16 and 19:23)- Spirit left him and he prophesied (respectively)

1 Samuel 16:14: But the Spirit of the LORD departed from Saul, and an evil spirit from the LORD troubled him.

1 Samuel 16:15: And Saul's servants said unto him, Behold now, an evil spirit from God troubleth thee.

1 Samuel 16:16: Let our lord now command thy servants, which are before thee, to seek out a man, who is a cunning player on an harp: and it shall come to pass, when the evil spirit from God is upon thee, that he shall play with his hand, and thou shalt be well.

1 Samuel 19:23: And he went thither to Naioth in Ramah: and the Spirit of God was upon him also, and he went on, and prophesied, until he came to Naioth in Ramah.

Messengers of Saul

(1 Samuel 19:20,21) – Prophesied

1 Samuel 19:20: And Saul sent messengers to take David: and when they saw the company of the prophets prophesying, and Samuel standing as appointed over them, the Spirit of God was upon the messengers of Saul, and they also prophesied.

1 Samuel 19:21: And when it was told Saul, he sent other messengers, and they prophesied likewise. And Saul sent messengers again the third time, and they prophesied also.

David

(1 Samuel 16:13, 2 Samuel 23:2, Mark 12:36 and Acts 1:16) – appointment of king, used him to speak

1 Samuel 16:13: Then Samuel took the horn of oil, and anointed him in the midst of his brethren: and the Spirit of the LORD came upon David from that day forward. So Samuel rose up, and went to Ramah.

2 Samuel 23:2: The Spirit of the LORD spake by me, and his word was in my tongue.

Mark 12:36: For David himself said by the Holy Ghost, The LORD said to my Lord, Sit thou on my right hand, till I make thine enemies thy footstool.

Acts 1:16: Men and brethren, this scripture must needs have been fulfilled, which the Holy Ghost by the mouth of David spake before concerning Judas, which was guide to them that took Jesus.

Obadiah

(1 Kings 18:12) - led him (per Elijah)

1 Kings 18:12: And it shall come to pass, as soon as I am gone from thee, that the Spirit of the LORD shall carry thee whither I know not; and so when I come and tell Ahab, and he cannot find thee, he shall slay me: but I thy servant fear the LORD from my youth.

Elijah and Elisha

(2 Kings 2:9,15)

2 Kings 2:9: And it came to pass, when they were gone over, that Elijah said unto Elisha, Ask what I shall do for thee, before I be taken away from thee. And Elisha said, I pray thee, let a double portion of thy spirit be upon me.

2 Kings 2:15: And when the sons of the prophets which were to view at Jericho saw him, they said, The spirit of Elijah doth rest on Elisha. And they came to meet him, and bowed themselves to the ground before him.

Amassi

(1 Chronicles 12:18) – declared allegiance to David

1 Chronicles 12:18: Then the spirit came upon Amasai, who was chief of the captains, and he said, Thine are we, David, and on thy side, thou son of Jesse: peace, peace be unto thee, and peace be to thine helpers; for thy God helpeth thee. Then David received them, and made them captains of the band.

Azariah

(2 Chronicles 15:1) – declared a message to Asa

2 Chronicles 15:1: And the Spirit of God came upon Azariah the son of Oded:

Jahaziel

(Levite)

(2 Chronicles 20:14) – spoke to Judah and Jehoshaphat

2 Chronicles 20:14: Then upon Jahaziel the son of Zechariah, the son of Benaiah, the son of Jeiel, the son of Mattaniah, a Levite of the sons of Asaph, came the Spirit of the LORD in the midst of the congregation;

Zechariah

(Levite)

(2 Chronicles 24:20) – spoke to the people

2 Chronicles 24:20: And the Spirit of God came upon Zechariah the son of Jehoiada the priest, which stood above the people, and said unto them, Thus saith God, Why transgress ye the commandments of the LORD, that ye cannot prosper? because ye have forsaken the LORD, he hath also forsaken you.

Daniel

(Daniel 4:8, 9, 18, 5:11) – revealed/interpreted dreams

Daniel 4:8: But at the last Daniel came in before me, whose name was Belteshazzar, according to the name of my god, and in whom is the spirit of the holy gods: and before him I told the dream, saying,

Daniel 4:9: O Belteshazzar, master of the magicians, because I know that the spirit of the holy gods is in thee, and no secret troubleth thee, tell me the visions of my dream that I have seen, and the interpretation thereof.

Daniel 4:18: This dream I king Nebuchadnezzar have seen. Now thou, O Belteshazzar, declare the interpretation thereof, forasmuch as all the wise men of my kingdom are not able to make known unto me the interpretation: but thou art able; for the spirit of the holy gods is in thee.

Daniel 5:11: There is a man in thy kingdom, in whom is the spirit of the holy gods; and in the days of thy father light and understanding and wisdom, like the wisdom of the gods, was found in him; whom the king

Nebuchadnezzar thy father, the king, I say, thy father, made master of the magicians, astrologers, Chaldeans, and soothsayers;

Isaiah

(Isaiah 61:1) – declared that the Spirit was upon him to bring freedom

Isaiah 61:1: The Spirit of the Lord GOD is upon me; because the LORD hath anointed me to preach good tidings unto the meek; he hath sent me to bind up the brokenhearted, to proclaim liberty to the captives, and the opening of the prison to them that are bound;

Ezekiel

(Levite)

(Ezekiel 2:2) – Began to hear from God
Ezekiel 2:2: And the spirit entered into me when he spake unto me, and set me upon my feet, that I heard him that spake unto me.

His vessels in the New Testament

Jesus

(conceived by the Spirit) – (Matthew 1:18, 20, Luke 1:26-35)

(Branch of Jesse) (Isaiah 11:2, Luke 4:18, Matthew 3:16, Mark 9:10, Acts 10:38) – the Spirit being upon Him,

I John 5:8: – He being the Word made flesh (John 1:14)

Matthew 1:18: Now the birth of Jesus Christ was on this wise: When as his mother Mary was espoused to Joseph, before they came together, she was found with child of the Holy Ghost.

Matthew 1:20: But while he thought on these things, behold, the angel of the Lord appeared unto him in a dream, saying, Joseph, thou son of David, fear not to take unto thee Mary thy wife: for that which is conceived in her is of the Holy Ghost.

Luke 1:26: And in the sixth month the angel Gabriel was sent from God unto a city of Galilee, named Nazareth,

Luke 1:27: To a virgin espoused to a man whose name was Joseph, of the house of David; and the virgin's name was Mary.

Luke 1:28: And the angel came in unto her, and said, Hail, thou that art highly favoured, the Lord is with thee: blessed art thou among women.

Luke 1:29: And when she saw him, she was troubled at his saying, and cast in her mind what manner of salutation this should be.

Luke 1:30: And the angel said unto her, Fear not, Mary: for thou hast found favour with God.

Luke 1:31: And, behold, thou shalt conceive in thy womb, and bring forth a son, and shalt call his name JESUS.

Luke 1:32: He shall be great, and shall be called the Son of the Highest: and the Lord God shall give unto him the throne of his father David:

Luke 1:33: And he shall reign over the house of Jacob for ever; and of his kingdom there shall be no end.

Luke 1:34: Then said Mary unto the angel, How shall this be, seeing I know not a man?

Luke 1:35: And the angel answered and said unto her, The Holy Ghost shall come upon thee, and the power of the Highest shall overshadow thee: therefore also that holy thing which shall be born of thee shall be called the Son of God.

Isaiah 11:2: And the spirit of the LORD shall rest upon him, the spirit of wisdom and understanding, the spirit of counsel and might, the spirit of knowledge and of the fear of the LORD;

Luke 4:18: The Spirit of the Lord is upon me, because he hath anointed me to preach the gospel to the poor; he hath sent me to heal the broken-hearted, to preach deliverance to the captives, and recovering of sight to the blind, to set at liberty them that are bruised,

Matthew 3:16: And Jesus, when he was baptized, went up straightway out of the water: and, lo, the heavens were opened unto him, and he saw the Spirit of God descending like a dove, and lighting upon him:

Mark 9:10: And they kept that saying with themselves, questioning one with another what the rising from the dead should mean.

Acts 10:38: How God anointed Jesus of Nazareth with the Holy Ghost and with power: who went about doing good, and healing all that were oppressed of the devil; for God was with him.

1 John 5:8: And there are three that bear witness in earth, the Spirit, and the water, and the blood: and these three agree in one.

John 1:14: And the Word was made flesh, and dwelt among us, (and we beheld his glory, the glory as of the only begotten of the Father,) full of grace and truth.

Simeon

(Luke 2:25, 26) – Holy Ghost was upon him and by the Holy Ghost he found out that he would not see death until he saw Christ

Luke 2:25: And, behold, there was a man in Jerusalem, whose name was Simeon; and the same man was just and devout, waiting for the consolation of Israel: and the Holy Ghost was upon him.

Luke 2:26: And it was revealed unto him by the Holy Ghost, that he should not see death, before he had seen the Lord's Christ.

Disciples

(Acts 13:52) – filled (joy – see fruit)

Acts 13:52: And the disciples were filled with joy, and with the Holy Ghost.

Apostles and those in the upper room (120 total) (Acts 2:4) – Spoke in other tongues, brought thousands to Jesus

Acts 2:4: And they were all filled with the Holy Ghost, and began to speak with other tongues, as the Spirit gave them utterance.

Stephen

(Acts 6:5, 7:55) – full of the Holy Ghost. One of the respected seven.

Acts 6:5: And the saying pleased the whole multitude: and they chose Stephen, a man full of faith and of the Holy Ghost, and Philip, and Prochorus, and Nicanor, and Timon, and Parmenas, and Nicolas a proselyte of Antioch:

Acts 7:55: But he, being full of the Holy Ghost, looked up stedfastly into heaven, and saw the glory of God, and Jesus standing on the right hand of God,

Men who were appointed to handle ministration

(Acts 6:2-5)

Acts 6:2: Then the twelve called the multitude of the disciples unto them, and said, It is not reason that we should leave the word of God, and serve tables.

Acts 6:3: Wherefore, brethren, look ye out among you seven men of honest report, full of the Holy Ghost and wisdom, whom we may appoint over this business.

Acts 6:4: But we will give ourselves continually to prayer, and to the ministry of the word.

Acts 6:5: And the saying pleased the whole multitude: and they chose Stephen, a man full of faith and of the Holy Ghost, and Philip, and Prochorus, and Nicanor, and Timon, and Parmenas, and Nicolas a proselyte of Antioch:

Paul

(Acts 9:17, 13:9) filled with the Holy Ghost (1 Cor 13:1- tongues of angels)

Acts 9:17: And Ananias went his way, and entered into the house; and putting his hands on him said, Brother Saul, the Lord, even Jesus, that appeared unto thee in the way as thou camest, hath sent me, that thou mightest receive thy sight, and be filled with the Holy Ghost.

Acts 13:9: Then Saul, (who also is called Paul,) filled with the Holy Ghost, set his eyes on him,

1 Corinthians 13:1: Though I speak with the tongues of men and of angels, and have not charity, I am become as sounding brass, or a tinkling cymbal.

Phillip

(Acts 8:28, 29) Preached the kingdom of God and brought souls in, another of the respected seven

Acts 8:28: Was returning, and sitting in his chariot read Esaias the prophet.

Acts 8:29: Then the Spirit said unto Philip, Go near, and join thyself to this chariot.

Peter

(Acts 4:8, 10:19, 11:12) – Holy Spirit spoke to Peter about Cornelius, Led Peter

Acts 4:8: Then Peter, filled with the Holy Ghost, said unto them, Ye rulers of the people, and elders of Israel,

Acts 10:19: While Peter thought on the vision, the Spirit said unto him, Behold, three men seek thee.

Acts 11:12: And the Spirit bade me go with them, nothing doubting. Moreover these six brethren accompanied me, and we entered into the man's house:

Agabus

(Acts 11:28, 21:10) – prophesied

Acts 11:28: And there stood up one of them named Agabus, and signified by the Spirit that there should be great dearth throughout all the world: which came to pass in the days of Claudius Caesar.

Acts 21:10: And as we tarried there many days, there came down from Judaea a certain prophet, named Agabus.

Anna

Luke 2:36 And there was one Anna, a prophetess, the daughter of Phanuel, of the tribe of Aser: she was of a great age, and had lived with an husband seven years from her virginity;

Daughters of Phillip

(Acts 21:8-9) – prophesied

Acts 21:8: And the next day we that were of Paul's company departed, and came unto Caesarea: and we entered into the house of Philip the evangelist, which was one of the seven; and abode with him.

Acts 21:9: And the same man had four daughters, virgins, which did prophesy.

Mary

(Luke 1:35) – Jesus was conceived when the Holy Spirit overshadowed Mary's womb.

Luke 1:35: And the angel answered and said unto her, The Holy Ghost shall come upon thee, and the power of the Highest shall overshadow thee: therefore also that holy thing which shall be born of thee shall be called the Son of God.

Elisabeth

(Levite, from daughters of Aaron and Mother of **John the Baptist**)

Filled when a pregnant Mary came close to her (Luke 1:41) – was Mary's cousin, well in years and mother of whom Isaiah (Isaiah 40:3) prophesied (John).

Luke 1:41: And it came to pass, that, when Elisabeth heard the salutation of Mary, the babe leaped in her womb; and Elisabeth was filled with the Holy Ghost:

Isaiah 40:3: The voice of him that crieth in the wilderness, Prepare ye the way of the LORD, make straight in the desert a highway for our God.

John the Baptist

(Levite)

(Luke 1:13-17, 41) – John was filled in the womb when the baby Jesus came close.

Luke 1:13: But the angel said unto him, Fear not, Zacharias: for thy prayer is heard; and thy wife Elisabeth shall bear thee a son, and thou shalt call his name John.

Luke 1:14: And thou shalt have joy and gladness; and many shall rejoice at his birth.

Luke 1:15: For he shall be great in the sight of the Lord, and shall drink neither wine nor strong drink; and he shall be filled with the Holy Ghost, even from his mother's womb.

Luke 1:16: And many of the children of Israel shall he turn to the Lord their God.

Luke 1: 17: And he shall go before him in the spirit and power of Elias, to turn the hearts of the fathers to the children, and the disobedient to the wisdom of the just; to make ready a people prepared for the Lord.

Luke 1:41: And it came to pass, that, when Elisabeth heard the salutation of Mary, the babe leaped in her womb; and Elisabeth was filled with the Holy Ghost:

Zacharias

(Levite, father of John the Baptist)

(Luke 1:67) – prophesied

Luke 1:67: And his father Zacharias was filled with the Holy Ghost, and prophesied, saying,

Barnabas

(Levite)

(Acts 11:22-24) –full of the Holy Ghost and added souls to the Lord

Acts 11:22: Then tidings of these things came unto the ears of the church which was in Jerusalem: and they sent forth Barnabas, that he should go as far as Antioch.

Acts 11:23: Who, when he came, and had seen the grace of God, was glad, and exhorted them all, that with purpose of heart they would cleave unto the Lord.

Acts 11:24: For he was a good man, and full of the Holy Ghost and of faith: and much people was added unto the Lord.

Barnabas and Saul

(Acts 13:1-4) – Spirit spoke to the Church in Antioch and told them to release Barnabas and Saul for the work of God.

Acts 13:1: Now there were in the church that was at Antioch certain prophets and teachers; as Barnabas, and Simeon that was called Niger, and Lucius of Cyrene, and Manaen, which had been brought up with Herod the tetrarch, and Saul.

Acts 13:2: As they ministered to the Lord, and fasted, the Holy Ghost said, Separate me Barnabas and Saul for the work whereunto I have called them.

Acts 13:3: And when they had fasted and prayed, and laid their hands on them, they sent them away.

Acts 13:4: So they, being sent forth by the Holy Ghost, departed unto Seleucia; and from thence they sailed to Cyprus.

Twelve men of Acts 19

(Acts 19:6) - Spake with tongues and prophesied

Acts 19:6: And when Paul had laid his hands upon them, the Holy Ghost came on them; and they spake with tongues, and prophesied.

House of Cornelius

(Acts 10:44-46a, 11:15, 16, 15:8) Spake with tongues

Acts 10:44: While Peter yet spake these words, the Holy Ghost fell on all them which heard the word.

Acts 10:45: And they of the circumcision which believed were astonished, as many as came with Peter, because that on the Gentiles also was poured out the gift of the Holy Ghost.

Acts 10:46a: For they heard them speak with tongues, and magnify God.

Acts 11:15: And as I began to speak, the Holy Ghost fell on them, as on us at the beginning.

Acts 11:16: Then remembered I the word of the Lord, how that he said, John indeed baptized with water; but ye shall be baptized with the Holy Ghost.

Acts 15:8: And God, which knoweth the hearts, bare them witness, giving them the Holy Ghost, even as he did unto us;

VII.

Holy Spirit and His connection to Heaven and Earth

11

Holy Spirit and His Connection to Heaven and Earth

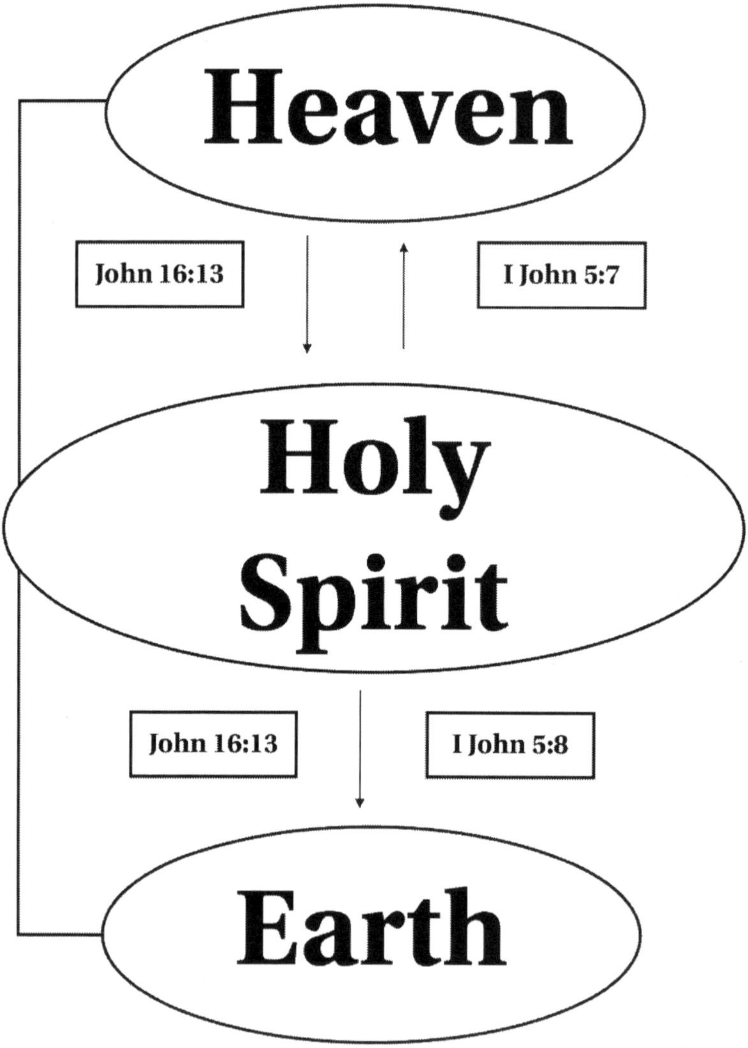

John 16:13: Howbeit when he, the Spirit of truth, is come, he will guide you into all truth: for he shall not speak of himself; but whatsoever he shall hear, *that* shall he speak: and he will shew you things to come.

1 John 5:7: For there are three that bear record in heaven, the Father, the Word, and the Holy Ghost: and these three are one.

1 John 5:8: And there are three that bear witness in earth, the Spirit, and the water, and the blood: and these three agree in one.

The Holy Spirit is our connection to heaven.

Embrace, receive, yield, and release and watch what He does!

VIII.

The PROMISE of the Spirit

12

The Promise of the Spirit

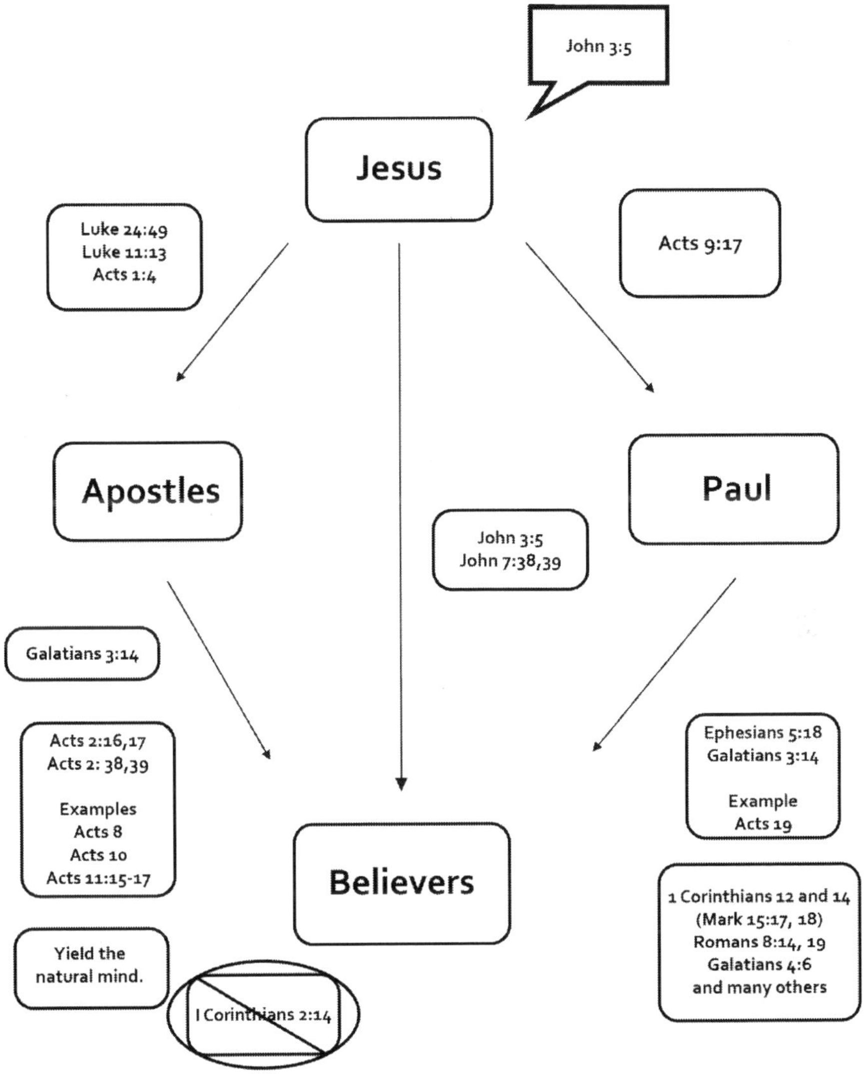

1 John 2:27: But the **anointing**[G5545] **which ye have received of him** [M3:11, L3:16] **abideth in you**[J14:17], and ye need not that any man teach you: but as **the same anointing teacheth you of all things**[J14:26]and **is truth**[J14:17], and is no lie, and even as it hath taught you, ye shall abide in him.

G5545 – charisma – Gift of the Holy Spirit,

Mark 3:11: And unclean spirits, when they saw him, fell down before him, and cried, saying, Thou art the Son of God.

Luke 3:16: John answered, saying unto them all, I indeed baptize you with water; but one mightier than I cometh, the latchet of whose shoes I am not worthy to unloose: he shall baptize you with the Holy Ghost and with fire:

John 14:17: Even the Spirit of truth; whom the world cannot receive, because it seeth him not, neither knoweth him: but ye know him; for he dwelleth with you, and shall be in you.

John 14:26: But the Comforter, which is the Holy Ghost, whom the Father will send in my name, he shall teach you all things, and bring all things to your remembrance, whatsoever I have said unto you.

Joel 2:28: And it shall come to pass afterward, that I will pour out my spirit upon all flesh; and your sons and your daughters shall prophesy, your old men shall dream dreams, your young men shall see visions:

Joel 2:29: And also upon the servants and upon the handmaids in those days will I pour out my spirit.

13

The Promise of the Spirit (Scriptures)

John 3:5: Jesus answered, Verily, verily, I say unto thee, Except a man be born of water and of the Spirit, he cannot enter into the kingdom of God.

Jesus to the Apostles

Luke 24:49: And, behold, I send the promise of my Father upon you: but tarry ye in the city of Jerusalem, until ye be endued with power from on high.

Luke 11:13: If ye then, being evil, know how to give good gifts unto your children: how much more shall your heavenly Father give the Holy Spirit to them that ask him?

Acts 1:4: And, being assembled together with them, commanded them that they should not depart from Jerusalem, but wait for the promise of the Father, which, saith he, ye have heard of me.

Jesus to Paul

Acts 9:17: And Ananias went his way, and entered into the house; and putting his hands on him said, Brother Saul, the Lord, even Jesus, that appeared unto thee in the way as thou camest, hath sent me, that thou mightest receive thy sight, and be filled with the Holy Ghost.

Jesus to all believers

John 3:5: Jesus answered, Verily, verily, I say unto thee, Except a man be born of water and of the Spirit, he cannot enter into the kingdom of God.

John 7:38: He that believeth on me, as the scripture hath said, out of his belly shall flow rivers of living water.

John 7:39: (But this spake he of the Spirit, which they that believe on him should receive: for the Holy Ghost was not yet given; because that Jesus was not yet glorified.)

Apostles to all believers

Acts 2:16: But this is that which was spoken by the prophet Joel;

Acts 2:17: And it shall come to pass in the last days, saith God, I will pour out of my Spirit upon all flesh: and your sons and your daughters shall prophesy, and your young men shall see visions, and your old men shall dream dreams:

Acts 2:38: Then Peter said unto them, Repent, and be baptized every one of you in the name of Jesus Christ for the remission of sins, and ye shall receive the gift of the Holy Ghost.

Acts 2:39: For the promise is unto you, and to your children, and to all that are afar off, even as many as the Lord our God shall call.

Galatians 3:14: That the blessing of Abraham might come on the Gentiles through Jesus Christ; that we might receive the promise of the Spirit through faith.

Examples: Read Acts 8, Acts 10 and Acts 11:15-17

Must yield the natural mind

1 Corinthians 2:14: But the natural man receiveth not the things of the Spirit of God: for they are foolishness unto him: neither can he know them, because they are spiritually discerned.

IX.

Is the Holy Spirit for me?

14

Is the Holy Spirit for me? (Letter)

Dear Holy Spirit:

Thank you. Thank you for showing us that You are for anyone and everyone who calls on You. There are so many of us out there who desire more in our relationship with God. We are hungry for something that we can not put our finger on. We desire Your guidance, Your wisdom, Your power, Your faith, Your knowledge and every single thing You offer and desire to give us severally as You will (1 Corinthian 12:11)

If anything, I want to show everyone reading this book that You are the direct connection to Heaven and the Earth, and if we want God's will on this Earth, we need to know what heaven says and what heaven wants.

We thank You for being available to us. We thank you for being patient with us. We thank you for allowing Jesus to send You to us. We thank You for wanting to be with us. For all things, we love You.

Love,
Your servant,
Marco

15

Is the Holy Spirit for me? (Scriptures)

The Promise (to the Apostles)

Luke 24:49: And, behold, I send the promise of my Father upon you: but tarry ye in the city of Jerusalem, until ye be endued with power from on high.

Acts 1:4: And, being assembled together with them, commanded them that they should not depart from Jerusalem, but wait for the promise of the Father, which, saith he, ye have heard of me.

Acts 1:5: For John truly baptized with water; but ye shall be baptized with the Holy Ghost not many days hence.

Acts 1:8: But ye shall receive power, after that the Holy Ghost is come upon you: and ye shall be witnesses unto me both in Jerusalem, and in all Judaea, and in Samaria, and unto the uttermost part of the earth.

Acts 2:33: Therefore being by the right hand of God exalted, and having received of the Father the promise of the Holy Ghost, he hath shed forth this, which ye now see and hear.

The Promise (to the people)

Acts 2:3: And there appeared unto them cloven tongues like as of fire, and it sat upon each of them.

Acts 2:4: And they were all filled with the Holy Ghost, and began to speak with other tongues, as the Spirit gave them utterance.

Acts 2:16: But this is that which was spoken by the prophet Joel;

Acts 2:17: And it shall come to pass in the last days, saith God, I will pour out of my Spirit upon **all** flesh: and your sons and your daughters shall prophesy, and your young men shall see visions, and your old men shall dream dreams:

Acts 2:38: Then Peter said unto them, Repent, and be baptized every one of you in the name of Jesus Christ for the remission of sins, and ye shall receive the gift of the Holy Ghost.

Acts 2:39: For the promise is unto you, and to your children, and to all that are afar off, even as many as the Lord our God shall call.

Galatians 3:14: That the blessing of Abraham might come on the Gentiles through Jesus Christ; that we might receive the promise of the Spirit through faith.

Ephesians 1:13: In whom ye also trusted, after that ye heard the word of truth, the gospel of your salvation: in whom also after that ye believed, ye were sealed with that holy Spirit of promise,

X.

How does the Holy Spirit come?

16

How does the Holy Spirit come? (Letter)

Dear Holy Spirit:

Oh, how do I remember them. Oh, how I remember the moments where I defended Your reality and Your necessity. Did I need to defend You in the court of earthly law? No. Did I need to defend You in the court of religious law? No. I had a great time doing the latter, but it was unnecessary.

In their defense, I realized that knowing how You became available and how You came into our lives is foreign to many. Why? So many people never address how important it is to have You in our lives. Many do not even know how to ask You to be in their lives.

I want this section to take us from the promise to the delivery, and then to the entrance after the invitation. In multiple examples there are common denominators that help us to receive You. Whether it was Paul, the Apostles or the others in the upper room or the house of Cornelius, I see a hunger and the desire to follow instructions whether they were given by men, by You, or directly through heaven.

You come when our hearts are ready for You to come. We thank You for answering every hungry heart out there.

Love,
Your Servant,
Marco

17

How does the Holy Spirit come? (Scriptures)

The Command

John 3:5: Jesus answered, Verily, verily, I say unto thee, Except a man be born of water and of the Spirit, he cannot enter into the kingdom of God.

Must be on one accord

Acts 2:1: And when the day of Pentecost was fully come, they were all with one accord in one place.

Acts 2:2: And suddenly there came a sound from heaven as of a rushing mighty wind, and it filled all the house where they were sitting.

Acts 2:3: And there appeared unto them cloven tongues like as of fire, and it sat upon each of them.

Acts 2:4: And they were all filled with the Holy Ghost, and began to speak with other tongues, as the Spirit gave them utterance.

Ask/Prayer by faith

Luke 11:13: If ye then, being evil, know how to give good gifts unto your children: how much more shall your heavenly Father give the Holy Spirit to them that ask him?

Acts 4:31: And when they had prayed, the place was shaken where they were assembled together; and they were all filled with the Holy Ghost, and they spake the word of God with boldness.

Acts 8:15: Who, when they were come down, prayed for them, that they might receive the Holy Ghost:

Galatians 3:2: This only would I learn of you, Received ye the Spirit by the works of the law, or by the hearing of faith?

Galatians 3:14: That the blessing of Abraham might come on the Gentiles through Jesus Christ; that we might receive the promise of the Spirit through faith.

Gift from God

John 14:16: And I will pray the Father, and he shall give you another Comforter, that he may abide with you for ever;

John 14:17: Even the Spirit of truth; whom the world cannot receive, because it seeth him not, neither knoweth him: but ye know him; for he dwelleth with you, and shall be in you.

John 14:16: And I will pray the Father, and he shall give you another Comforter, that he may abide with you for ever;

John 14:17: Even the Spirit of truth; whom the world cannot receive, because it seeth him not, neither knoweth him: but ye know him; for he dwelleth with you, and shall be in you.

John 14:17: Even the Spirit of truth; whom the world cannot receive, because it seeth him not, neither knoweth him: but ye know him; for he dwelleth with you, and shall be in you.

John 15:26: But when the Comforter is come, whom I will send unto you from the Father, even the Spirit of truth, which proceedeth from the Father, he shall testify of me:

Matthew 3:11: I indeed baptize you with water unto repentance: but he that cometh after me is mightier than I, whose shoes I am not worthy to bear: he shall baptize you with the Holy Ghost, and with fire:

Acts 2:16: But this is that which was spoken by the prophet Joel;

Acts 2:17: And it shall come to pass in the last days, saith God, I will pour out of my Spirit upon all flesh: and your sons and your daughters shall prophesy, and your young men shall see visions, and your old men shall dream dreams:

Laying on of Hands

Matthew 18:19: Again I say unto you, That if two of you shall agree on earth as touching any thing that they shall ask, it shall be done for them of my Father which is in heaven.

1 Timothy 4:14: Neglect not the gift that is in thee, which was given thee by prophecy, with the laying on of the hands of the presbytery. (gift here is the same word charisma (5486) used in I Corinthians 12:4)

Presbytery (G4244) (Thayer's) – body of elders, presbytery, senate, council. Of the elders of any body (church) of Christians

Charisma (G5486) (Thayer's) – extraordinary powers, distinguishing certain Christians and enabling them to serve the church of Christ, the reception of which is due to the power of divine grace operating in their souls by the Holy Spirit. specifically (I Tim 4:14) the sum of those powers requisite for the discharge of the office of an evangelist.

Apostles

Acts 8:17: Then laid they their hands on them, and they received the Holy Ghost.

Acts 19:6: And when Paul had laid his hands upon them, the Holy Ghost came on them; and they spake with tongues, and prophesied.

Ananias, a disciple

Acts 9:17: And Ananias went his way, and entered into the house; and putting his hands on him said, Brother Saul, the Lord, even Jesus, that appeared unto thee in the way as thou camest, hath sent me, that thou mightest receive thy sight, and be filled with the Holy Ghost.

Acts 9:18: And immediately there fell from his eyes as it had been scales: and he received sight forthwith, and arose, and was baptized.

Outpouring/Fell

Acts 2:2: And suddenly there came a sound from heaven as of a rushing mighty wind, and it filled all the house where they were sitting.

Acts 2:3: And there appeared unto them cloven tongues like as of fire, and it sat upon each of them.

Acts 2:4: And they were all filled with the Holy Ghost, and began to speak with other tongues, as the Spirit gave them utterance.

Acts 10:44: While Peter yet spake these words, the Holy Ghost fell on all them which heard the word. [Note how Peter states Acts 10:34: Then Peter opened his mouth, and said, Of a truth I perceive that God is no respecter of persons: and how those of circumcision were astonished at this outpouring (Acts 10:45) and how Peter states that the Holy Ghost fell on them as on us (Acts 11:15)]

Around Baptism

(post or pre-water baptism) (Note how the births that Jesus spoke of John 3:5 work hand in hand) (Part W = water, Part HS = Holy Spirit)

Part W (water) + HS (Holy Spirit)

Acts 2:38: Then Peter said unto them, Repent, and be baptized every one of you in the name of Jesus Christ for the remission of sins, and ye shall receive the gift of the Holy Ghost.

Part W (water with Phillip), Part HS (Holy Spirit with Peter and John)

Acts 8:12: But when they believed Philip preaching the things concerning the kingdom of God, and the name of Jesus Christ, they were baptized, both men and women.

Acts 8:14: Now when the apostles which were at Jerusalem heard that Samaria had received the word of God, they sent unto them Peter and John:

Acts 8:15: Who, when they were come down, prayed for them, that they might receive the Holy Ghost:

Acts 8:16: (For as yet he was fallen upon none of them: only they were baptized in the name of the Lord Jesus.)

Acts 8:17: Then laid they their hands on them, and they received the Holy Ghost.

Part HS (Holy Spirit) then Part W (Water)

Acts 10:44: While Peter yet spake these words, the Holy Ghost fell on all them which heard the word.

Acts 10:45: And they of the circumcision which believed were astonished, as many as came with Peter, because that on the Gentiles also was poured out the gift of the Holy Ghost.

Acts 10:46: For they heard them speak with tongues, and magnify God. Then answered Peter,

Acts 10:47: Can any man forbid water, that these should not be baptized, which have received the Holy Ghost as well as we?

Acts 10:48: And he commanded them to be baptized in the name of the Lord. Then prayed they him to tarry certain days.

Part W (Water) and Part HS (Holy Spirit) with Paul

Acts 19:5: When they heard this, they were baptized in the name of the Lord Jesus.

Acts 19:6: And when Paul had laid his hands upon them, the Holy Ghost came on them; and they spake with tongues, and prophesied.

Acts 19:7: And all the men were about twelve.

Part W (Water) and Part HS (Holy Spirit) with Paul and Ananias

Acts 9:10: And there was a certain disciple at Damascus, named Ananias; and to him said the Lord in a vision, Ananias. And he said, Behold, I am here, Lord.

Acts 9:11: And the Lord said unto him, Arise, and go into the street which is called Straight, and enquire in the house of Judas for one called Saul, of Tarsus: for, behold, he prayeth,

Acts 9:12: And hath seen in a vision a man named Ananias coming in, and putting his hand on him, that he might receive his sight.

Acts 9:13: Then Ananias answered, Lord, I have heard by many of this man, how much evil he hath done to thy saints at Jerusalem:

Acts 9:14: And here he hath authority from the chief priests to bind all that call on thy name.

Acts 9:15: But the Lord said unto him, Go thy way: for he is a chosen vessel unto me, to bear my name before the Gentiles, and kings, and the children of Israel:

Acts 9:16: For I will shew him how great things he must suffer for my name's sake.

Acts 9:17: And Ananias went his way, and entered into the house; and putting his hands on him said, Brother Saul, the Lord, even Jesus, that appeared unto thee in the way as thou camest, hath sent me, that thou mightest receive thy sight, and be filled with the Holy Ghost.

Acts 9:18: And immediately there fell from his eyes as it had been scales: and he received sight forthwith, and arose, and was baptized.

Acts 22:12: And one Ananias, a devout man according to the law, having a good report of all the Jews which dwelt there,

Acts 22:13: Came unto me, and stood, and said unto me, Brother Saul, receive thy sight. And the same hour I looked up upon him.

Acts 22:14: And he said, The God of our fathers hath chosen thee, that thou shouldest know his will, and see that Just One, and shouldest hear the voice of his mouth.

Acts 22:15: For thou shalt be his witness unto all men of what thou hast seen and heard.

Acts 22:16: And now why tarriest thou? arise, and be baptized, and wash away thy sins, calling on the name of the Lord.

XI.

Thoughts from Paul on the Holy Spirit

18

Thoughts from Paul on the Holy Spirit (Letter)

Dear Friend in Christ:

This section is all "Paul". This section shares passages where he encourages the church to embrace the Holy Spirit and tells those in the church just how important He is and why He needs to be in our lives. We thank the Apostle Paul for being the vessel we needed to share about the Spirit we need.

Your friend in Christ,
Marco

19

Thoughts from Paul on the Holy Spirit (Scriptures)

Acts 19:2: He said unto them, Have ye received the Holy Ghost since ye believed? And they said unto him, We have not so much as heard whether there be any Holy Ghost.

Acts 19:6: And when Paul had laid his hands upon them, the Holy Ghost came on them; and they spake with tongues, and prophesied.

Romans 5:5: And hope maketh not ashamed; because the love of God is shed abroad in our hearts by the Holy Ghost which is given unto us.

Romans 8:1: There is therefore now no condemnation to them which are in Christ Jesus, who walk not after the flesh, but after the Spirit.

Romans 8:2: For the law of the Spirit of life in Christ Jesus hath made me free from the law of sin and death.

Romans 8:4: That the righteousness of the law might be fulfilled in us, who walk not after the flesh, but after the Spirit.

Romans 8:5: For they that are after the flesh do mind the things of the flesh; but they that are after the Spirit the things of the Spirit.
Romans 8:9: But ye are not in the flesh, but in the Spirit, if so be that the Spirit of God dwell in you. Now if any man have not the Spirit of Christ, he is none of his.

Romans 8:10: And if Christ be in you, the body is dead because of sin; but the Spirit is life because of righteousness.

Romans 8:11: But if the Spirit of him that raised up Jesus from the dead dwell in you, he that raised up Christ from the dead shall also quicken your mortal bodies by his Spirit that dwelleth in you.

Romans 8:14: For as many as are led by the Spirit of God, they are the sons of God.

Romans 8:15: For ye have not received the spirit of bondage again to fear; but ye have received the Spirit of adoption, whereby we cry, Abba, Father.

Roans 8:16: The Spirit itself beareth witness with our spirit, that we are the children of God:

Romans 8:26: Likewise the Spirit also helpeth our infirmities: for we know not what we should pray for as we ought: but the Spirit itself maketh intercession for us with groanings which cannot be uttered.

Romans 8:27: And he that searcheth the hearts knoweth what is the mind of the Spirit, because he maketh intercession for the saints according to the will of God.

Romans 14:17: For the kingdom of God is not meat and drink; but righteousness, and peace, and joy in the Holy Ghost.

Romans 15:13: Now the God of hope fill you with all joy and peace in believing, that ye may abound in hope, through the power of the Holy Ghost.

Romans 15:16: That I should be the minister of Jesus Christ to the Gentiles, ministering the gospel of God, that the offering up of the Gentiles might be acceptable, being sanctified by the Holy Ghost.

1 Corinthians 2:4: And my speech and my preaching was not with enticing words of man's wisdom, but in demonstration of the Spirit and of power:

1 Corinthians 2:10: But God hath revealed them unto us by his Spirit: for the Spirit searcheth all things, yea, the deep things of God.

1 Corinthians 2:11: For what man knoweth the things of a man, save the spirit of man which is in him? even so the things of God knoweth no man, but the Spirit of God.

1 Corinthians 2:12: Now we have received, not the spirit of the world, but the spirit which is of God; that we might know the things that are freely given to us of God.

1 Corinthians 2:13: Which things also we speak, not in the words which man's wisdom teacheth, but which the Holy Ghost teacheth; comparing spiritual things with spiritual.

1 Corinthians 2:14: But the natural man receiveth not the things of the Spirit of God: for they are foolishness unto him: neither can he know them, because they are spiritually discerned.

1 Corinthians 3:16: Know ye not that ye are the temple of God, and that the Spirit of God dwelleth in you?

1 Corinthians 6:11: And such were some of you: but ye are washed, but ye are sanctified, but ye are justified in the name of the Lord Jesus, and by the Spirit of our God.

1 Corinthians 6:19: What? know ye not that your body is the temple of the Holy Ghost which is in you, which ye have of God, and ye are not your own?

1 Corinthians 12:3: Wherefore I give you to understand, that no man speaking by the Spirit of God calleth Jesus accursed: and that no man can say that Jesus is the Lord, but by the Holy Ghost.

1 Corinthians 12:4: Now there are diversities of gifts, but the same Spirit.

1 Corinthians 12:7: But the manifestation of the Spirit is given to every man to profit withal.

1 Corinthians 12:13: For by one Spirit are we all baptized into one body, whether we be Jews or Gentiles, whether we be bond or free; and have been all made to drink into one Spirit.

2 Corinthians 3:6: Who also hath made us able ministers of the new testament; not of the letter, but of the spirit: for the letter killeth, but the spirit giveth life.

2 Corinthians 3:17: Now the Lord is that Spirit: and where the Spirit of the Lord is, there is liberty.

2 Corinthians 3:18: But we all, with open face beholding as in a glass the glory of the Lord, are changed into the same image from glory to glory, even as by the Spirit of the Lord.

2 Corinthians 6:6: By pureness, by knowledge, by longsuffering, by kindness, by the Holy Ghost, by love unfeigned,

2 Corinthians 13:14: The grace of the Lord Jesus Christ, and the love of God, and the communion of the Holy Ghost, be with you all. Amen.
Galatians 3:2: This only would I learn of you, Received ye the Spirit by the works of the law, or by the hearing of faith?

Galatians 3:3: Are ye so foolish? having begun in the Spirit, are ye now made perfect by the flesh?

Galatians 3:5: He therefore that ministereth to you the Spirit, and worketh miracles among you, doeth he it by the works of the law, or by the hearing of faith?

Galatians 3:14: That the blessing of Abraham might come on the Gentiles through Jesus Christ; that we might receive the promise of the Spirit through faith.

Galatians 5:5: For we through the Spirit wait for the hope of righteousness by faith.

Galatians 5:16: This I say then, Walk in the Spirit, and ye shall not fulfil the lust of the flesh.

Galatians 5:17: For the flesh lusteth against the Spirit, and the Spirit against the flesh: and these are contrary the one to the other: so that ye cannot do the things that ye would.

Galatians 5:18: But if ye be led of the Spirit, ye are not under the law.

Galatians 5:22: But the fruit of the Spirit is love, joy, peace, longsuffering, gentleness, goodness, faith,

Galatians 5:23: Meekness, temperance: against such there is no law.

Galatians 5:25: If we live in the Spirit, let us also walk in the Spirit.

Galatians 6:8: For he that soweth to his flesh shall of the flesh reap corruption; but he that soweth to the Spirit shall of the Spirit reap life everlasting.

Ephesians 1:13: In whom ye also trusted, after that ye heard the word of truth, the gospel of your salvation: in whom also after that ye believed, ye were sealed with that holy Spirit of promise,

Ephesians 2:18: For through him we both have access by one Spirit unto the Father.

Ephesians 2:22: In whom ye also are builded together for an habitation of God through the Spirit.

Ephesians 3:16: That he would grant you, according to the riches of his glory, to be strengthened with might by his Spirit in the inner man;

Ephesians 4:30: And grieve not the holy Spirit of God, whereby ye are sealed unto the day of redemption.

Ephesians 5:9: (For the fruit of the Spirit is in all goodness and righteousness and truth;)

Ephesians 5:18: And be not drunk with wine, wherein is excess; but be filled with the Spirit;

Ephesians 6:17: And take the helmet of salvation, and the sword of the Spirit, which is the word of God:

Ephesians 6:18: Praying always with all prayer and supplication in the Spirit, and watching thereunto with all perseverance and supplication for all saints;

1 Thessalonians 1:5: For our gospel came not unto you in word only, but also in power, and in the Holy Ghost, and in much assurance; as ye know what manner of men we were among you for your sake.

1 Thessalonians 1:6: And ye became followers of us, and of the Lord, having received the word in much affliction, with joy of the Holy Ghost:

1 Thessalonians 4:8: He therefore that despiseth, despiseth not man, but God, who hath also given unto us his holy Spirit.

1 Thessalonians 5:19: Quench not the Spirit.

2 Timothy 1:14: That good thing which was committed unto thee keep by the Holy Ghost which dwelleth in us.

Titus 3:5: Not by works of righteousness which we have done, but according to his mercy he saved us, by the washing of regeneration, and renewing of the Holy Ghost;

Hebrews 2:4: God also bearing them witness, both with signs and wonders, and with divers miracles, and gifts of the Holy Ghost, according to his own will?

Hebrews 3:7: Wherefore (as the Holy Ghost saith, To day if ye will hear his voice,

Hebrews 6:4: For it is impossible for those who were once enlightened, and have tasted of the heavenly gift, and were made partakers of the Holy Ghost,

Hebrews 6:5: And have tasted the good word of God, and the powers of the world to come,

Hebrews 6:6: If they shall fall away, to renew them again unto repentance; seeing they crucify to themselves the Son of God afresh, and put him to an open shame.

Hebrews 10:15: Whereof the Holy Ghost also is a witness to us: for after that he had said before,

Hebrews 10:16: This is the covenant that I will make with them after those days, saith the Lord, I will put my laws into their hearts, and in their minds will I write them;

Hebrews 10:17: And their sins and iniquities will I remember no more.

XII.

Holy Spirit vs. other spirits

20

Holy Spirit vs. other spirits (Letter)

Dear Friend in Christ:

Before you dive into this section, I would like to share the following passage.

Ephesians 6:12: For we wrestle not against flesh and blood, but against principalities, against powers, against the rulers of the darkness of this world, against spiritual wickedness in high *places*.

Power. We have access to a Spirit of power (2 Timothy 1:7) who offers protection and deliverance from every spirit listed and unlisted. Since they are spirits, He gives us discernment (I Corinthian 12:10) and will reveal their actions and their entry points. It is very important to know the following and have quick and easy access to information that can change lives. Commit the following pages to memory and to your spirit. When you pray, thank the Holy Spirit for being (healing, peace, truth etc.) who cancels the assignments of the spirit of (heaviness, haughtiness, etc.,) and proclaim victory.

Now go and conquer.

Your friend in Christ,
Marco

21

Holy Spirit vs other spirits (Methods of operation)

Holy Spirit (through OUR direct and persistent invitation)		Other spirits (uninvited [through sin]/ persistent and aggresive)	
Adoption/ Dwell with	**Dwell inside/ Filled**	**Possession (body)**	**Oppression (mind)**
Romans 8:15 John 14:17	1 Corinthians 3:16 Ephesians 5:18 John 14:17	Matthew 4:24 Acts 8:7 Acts 16:16 Matthew 8:16 Matthew 8:23 Matthew 8:33 Matthew 9:32 Mark 1:32 Mark 5:15, 16 Mark 5:18 Luke 8:36	Acts 10:38

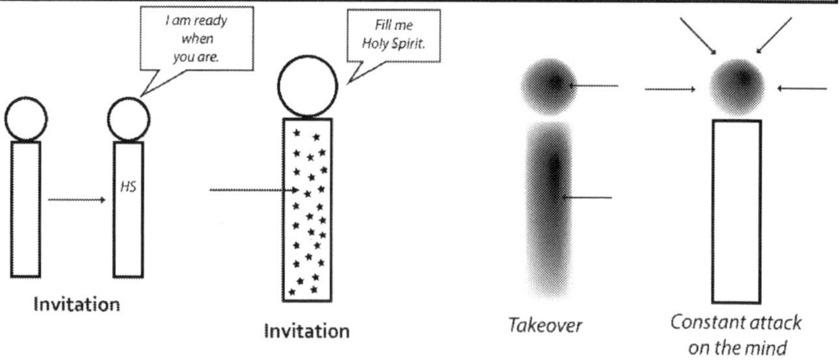

Holy Spirit - (Through a direct and constant conversation)

Adoption/Dwell with

Romans 8:15: For ye have not received the spirit of bondage again to fear; but ye have received the Spirit of adoption, whereby we cry, Abba, Father.

John 14:17: Even the Spirit of truth; whom the world cannot receive, because it seeth him not, neither knoweth him: but ye know him; for he dwelleth with you, and shall be in you.

Dwell inside/Filled

1 Corinthians 3:16: Know ye not that ye are the temple of God, and that the Spirit of God dwelleth in you?

Ephesians 5:18: And be not drunk with wine, wherein is excess; but be filled with the Spirit;

John 14:17: Even the Spirit of truth; whom the world cannot receive, because it seeth him not, neither knoweth him: but ye know him; for he dwelleth with you, and shall be in you.

Other spirits - (uninvited [through sin]/persistent and aggressive)

Possession

Matthew 4:24: And his fame went throughout all Syria: and they brought unto him all sick people that were taken with divers diseases and torments, and those which were possessed with devils, and those which were lunatick, and those that had the palsy; and he healed them.

Acts 8:7: For unclean spirits, crying with loud voice, came out of many that were possessed with them: and many taken with palsies, and that were lame, were healed.

Acts 16:16: And it came to pass, as we went to prayer, a certain damsel possessed with a spirit of divination met us, which brought her masters much gain by soothsaying:

Matthew 8:16: When the even was come, they brought unto him many that were possessed with devils: and he cast out the spirits with his word, and healed all that were sick:

Matthew 8:28: And when he was come to the other side into the country of the Gergesenes, there met him two possessed with devils, coming out of the tombs, exceeding fierce, so that no man might pass by that way.

Matthew 8:33: And they that kept them fled, and went their ways into the city, and told every thing, and what was befallen to the possessed of the devils.

Matthew 9:32: As they went out, behold, they brought to him a dumb man possessed with a devil.

Matthew 12:22: Then was brought unto him one possessed with a devil, blind, and dumb: and he healed him, insomuch that the blind and dumb both spake and saw.

Mark 1:32: And at even, when the sun did set, they brought unto him all that were diseased, and them that were possessed with devils.

Mark 5:15: And they come to Jesus, and see him that was possessed with the devil, and had the legion, sitting, and clothed, and in his right mind: and they were afraid.

Mark 5:16: And they that saw it told them how it befell to him that was possessed with the devil, and also concerning the swine.

Mark 5:18: And when he was come into the ship, he that had been possessed with the devil prayed him that he might be with him.

Luke 8:36: They also which saw it told them by what means he that was possessed of the devils was healed.

Oppression

Acts 10:38: How God anointed Jesus of Nazareth with the Holy Ghost and with power: who went about doing good, and healing all that were oppressed of the devil; for God was with him.

22

Holy Spirit vs. other Spirits (Scriptures)

The following is a biblical introduction of the spiritual war that Paul speaks of in Ephesians 6:12. May the following remind Christians who they have access to, what they are up against, and how to open the prisons to those who are bound (Isaiah 61:1).

The Holy Spirit

Galatians 3:14: That the blessing of Abraham might come on the Gentiles through Jesus Christ; that we might receive the promise of the Spirit through faith.

Acts 2:38: Then Peter said unto them, Repent, and be baptized every one of you in the name of Jesus Christ for the remission of sins, and ye shall receive the gift of the Holy Ghost.

Acts 2:39: For the promise is unto you, and to your children, and to all that are afar off, even as many as the Lord our God shall call.

Luke 11:13: If ye then, being evil, know how to give good gifts unto your children: how much more shall your heavenly Father give the Holy Spirit to them that ask him?

John 7:38: He that believeth on me, as the scripture hath said, out of his belly shall flow rivers of living water.

John 7:39: (But this spake he of the Spirit, which they that believe on him should receive: for the Holy Ghost was not yet given; because that Jesus was not yet glorified.)

Zechariah 4:6: Then he answered and spake unto me, saying, This is the word of the LORD unto Zerubbabel, saying, Not by might, nor by power, but by my spirit, saith the LORD of hosts.

2 Timothy 1:7: For God hath not given us the spirit of fear; but of power, and of love, and of a sound mind.

Isaiah 59:19: So shall they fear the name of the LORD from the west, and his glory from the rising of the sun. When the enemy shall come in like a flood, the Spirit of the LORD shall lift up a standard against him.

Romans 8:26: Likewise the Spirit also helpeth our infirmities: for we know not what we should pray for as we ought: but the Spirit itself maketh intercession for us with groanings which cannot be uttered.

John 16:13: Howbeit when he, the Spirit of truth, is come, he will guide you into all truth: for he shall not speak of himself; but whatsoever he shall hear, that shall he speak: and he will shew you things to come.

Our authority/weaponry over the devil and his minions.

Matthew 18:18: Verily I say unto you, Whatsoever ye shall bind on earth shall be bound in heaven: and whatsoever ye shall loose on earth shall be loosed in heaven.

James 4:7: Submit yourselves therefore to God. Resist the devil, and he will flee from you.

Luke 10:19: Behold, I give unto you power to tread on serpents and scorpions, and over all the power of the enemy: and nothing shall by any means hurt you.

Luke 10:20: Notwithstanding in this rejoice not, that the spirits are subject unto you; but rather rejoice, because your names are written in heaven.

James 2:19: Thou believest that there is one God; thou doest well: the devils also believe, and tremble.

2 Corinthians 10:3: For though we walk in the flesh, we do not war after the flesh:

2 Corinthians 10:4: (For the weapons of our warfare are not carnal, but mighty through God to the pulling down of strong holds;)

Ephesians 6:10: Finally, my brethren, be strong in the Lord, and in the power of his might.

Ephesians 6:11: Put on the whole armour of God, that ye may be able to stand against the wiles of the devil.

Ephesians 6:12: For we wrestle not against flesh and blood, but against principalities, against powers, against the rulers of the darkness of this world, against spiritual wickedness in high places.

Ephesians 6:13: Wherefore take unto you the whole armour of God, that ye may be able to withstand in the evil day, and having done all, to stand.

Ephesians 6:14: Stand therefore, having your loins girt about with truth, and having on the breastplate of righteousness;

Ephesians 6:15: And your feet shod with the preparation of the gospel of peace;

Ephesians 6:16: Above all, taking the shield of faith, wherewith ye shall be able to quench all the fiery darts of the wicked.

Ephesians 6:17: And take the helmet of salvation, and the sword of the Spirit, which is the word of God:

Ephesians 6:18: Praying always with all prayer and supplication in the Spirit, and watching thereunto with all perseverance and supplication for all saints;

Mark 9:23: Jesus said unto him, If thou canst believe, all things are possible to him that believeth.

Mark 9:28: And when he was come into the house, his disciples asked him privately, Why could not we cast him out?

Mark 9:29: And he said unto them, This kind can come forth by nothing, but by prayer and fasting.

John 14:13: And whatsoever ye shall ask in my name, that will I do, that the Father may be glorified in the Son.

John 14:14: If ye shall ask any thing in my name, I will do it.

Luke 10:17: And the seventy returned again with joy, saying, Lord, even the devils are subject unto us through thy name.

The tricks

2 Corinthians 11:14: And no marvel; for Satan himself is transformed into an angel of light.

Matthew 12:43: When the unclean spirit is gone out of a man, he walketh through dry places, seeking rest, and findeth none.

Matthew 12:44: Then he saith, I will return into my house from whence I came out; and when he is come, he findeth it empty, swept, and garnished.

Matthew 12:45: Then goeth he, and taketh with himself seven other spirits more wicked than himself, and they enter in and dwell there: and the last state of that man is worse than the first. Even so shall it be also unto this wicked generation.

1 Peter 5:8: Be sober, be vigilant; because your adversary the devil, as a roaring lion, walketh about, seeking whom he may devour:

Know the Spirit/spirit

1 Corinthians 12:10: …to another discerning of spirits…

1 John 4:1: Beloved, believe not every spirit, but try the spirits whether they are of God: because many false prophets are gone out into the world.

1 Corinthians 12:7: But the manifestation of the Spirit is given to every man to profit withal.

John 16:13: Howbeit when he, the Spirit of truth, is come, he will guide you into all truth: for he shall not speak of himself; but whatsoever he shall hear, that shall he speak: and he will shew you things to come.

23

Spirit of Adoption/Liberty vs. bondage

Holy Spirit and His gifts/fruit	VS.	The other spirits
Spirit of Adoption		**spirit of bondage**
Romans 8:15: **For ye have not received the spirit of bondage again to fear; but ye have received the Spirit of adoption, whereby we cry, Abba, Father.**	**VS.**	**Romans 8:15:** **For ye have not received the spirit of bondage again to fear; but ye have received the Spirit of adoption, whereby we cry, Abba, Father.**
Spirit of Liberty		
2 Corinthians 3:17: **Now the Lord is that Spirit: and where the Spirit of the Lord is, there is liberty.**		

24

Spirit of a Sound Mind/Faith vs. fear

Holy Spirit and His gifts/fruit	VS.	The other spirits
Spirit of a Sound Mind		spirit of fear
II Timothy 1:7 For God hath not given us a spirit of fear; but of power, and of love, and of a sound mind.		
Spirit of Faith		II Timothy 1:7 For God hath not given us a spirit of fear; but of power, and of love, and of a sound mind.
I Corinthians 12:9 To another faith by the same Spirit; II Corinthians 4:13 We having the same spirit of faith Galatians 5:22 But the fruit of the Spirit is love, joy, peace, longsuffering, gentleness, goodness faith,	VS.	

25

Spirit of Sound Mind/Joy/ Peace/ Liberty vs. heaviness

<table>
<tr><th>Holy Spirit and
His gifts/fruit</th><th>VS.</th><th>The other spirits</th></tr>
<tr><td>Spirit of a sound mind</td><td></td><td>spirit of heaviness</td></tr>
<tr><td>2 Timothy 1:7:

For God hath not given
us a spirit of fear;
but of power,
and of love,
and of a sound mind.</td><td rowspan="5">VS.</td><td rowspan="5">Isaiah 61:3:

To appoint unto them
that mourn in Zion,
to give unto them
beauty for ashes,
the oil of joy for
mourning,
the garment of praise
for the spirit
of heaviness.</td></tr>
<tr><td>Spirit of Joy/Peace</td></tr>
<tr><td>Galatians 5:22:

But the fruit of the Spirit
is love, joy, peace,
longsuffering, gentleness,
goodness, faith

Galatians 5:23:

Meekness, temperance:
against such there is no law</td></tr>
<tr><td>Spirit of Liberty</td></tr>
<tr><td>2 Corinthians 3:17:

Now the Lord is that
Spirit: and where the
Spirit of the Lord is,
there is liberty.</td></tr>
</table>

26

Spirit of Healing/Miracles vs. infirmity

Holy Spirit and His gifts/fruit	VS.	The other spirits
Spirit of Healing/Miracles		spirit of infirmity
1 Corinthians 12:9: ...to another the gifts of healing by the same Spirit; 1 Corinithians 12:10: To another the working of miracles; Romans 8:26: Likewise the Spirit also helpeth our infirmites: for we know not what we should pray for as we ought: but the Spirit itself maketh intercession for us with groanings which cannot be uttered.	VS.	Luke 13:11: And, behold, there was a woman which had a spirit of infirmity eighteen years, and was bowed together, and could in no wise lift up herself.

27

Spirit of Love vs. jealousy

Holy Spirit and His gifts/fruit	VS.	The other spirits
Spirit of Love	VS.	spirit of jealousy
Galatians 5:22: But the fruit of the Spirit is love, joy, peace longsuffering, gentleness goodness, faith, Galatians 5:23: Meekness, temperance: against such there is no law.		Numbers 5:14: And the spirit of jealousy come upon him, ... or if the spirit of jealousy come upon him, ...

28

Temple of the Holy Spirit/Renewed Mind vs. perverse spirit

Holy Spirit and His gifts/fruit	VS.	The other spirits
Temple of the Holy Ghost		perverse spirit
1 Corinthians 6:18: Flee fornication. Every sin that a man doeth is without the body; but he that committeth fornication sinneth against his own body. 1 Corinthians 6:19: What? know ye not that your body is the temple of the Holy Ghost which is in you, which ye have of God, and ye are not your own? 1 Corinthians 6:20: For ye are bought with a price: therefore glorify God in your body, and in your spirit, which are God's.	VS.	Isaiah 19:14: The LORD hath mingled a perverse spirit in the midst thereof: and they have caused Egypt to err in every work thereof, as a drunken man staggeth in his vomit.

Holy Spirit and His gifts/fruit	VS.	The other spirits
Renewed Mind		perverse spirit
Ephesians 4:23 And be renewed in the spirit of your mind;		Isaiah 19:14 The LORD hath mingled a perverse spirit in the midst thereof: and they have caused Egypt to err in every work thereof, as a drunken man staggeth in his vomit.
No lust	VS.	
Galatians 5:16 This I say then, Walk in the Spirit, and ye shall not fulfil the lust of the flesh. Galatians 5:17 For the flesh lusteth against the Spirit, and the Spirit against the flesh: and these are contrary the one to the other: so that ye cannot do the things that ye would.		

29

Spirit of Prophecy vs. divination/familiar spirit

Holy Spirit and His gifts/fruit	VS.	The other spirits
Spirit of Prophecy	VS.	spirit of divination and familiar spirit
1 Corinthians 12:10: To another the working of miracles; to another prophecy; to another discerning of spirits; to another divers kinds of tongues; to another the interpretation of tongues:		Acts 16:16: And it came to pass as we went to prayer, a certain damsel possessed with a spirit of divination met us, which brought her masters much gain by soothsaying: Leviticus 20:27: A man also or woman hath a familiar spirit...

30

Temple of the Holy Spirit vs. spirit of whoredoms

Holy Spirit and His gifts/fruit	VS.	The other spirits
Temple of the Holy Ghost		spirit of whoredoms
1 Corinthians 6:18: Flee fornication. Every sin that a man doeth is without the body; but he that committeth fornication sinneth against his own body. 1 Corinthians 6:19: What? know ye not that your body is the temple of the Holy Ghost which is in you, which ye have of God, and ye are not your own? 1 Corinthians 6:20: For ye are bought with a price: therefore glorify God in your body, and in your spirit, which are God's.	VS.	Hosea 4:12: My people ask counsel at their stocks, and their staff declareth unto them: for the spirit of whoredoms hath caused them to err, and they have gone a whoring from under their God.

31

Spirit of Meekness/Temperance (humility) vs. haughtiness (pride)

Holy Spirit and His gifts/fruit	VS.	The other spirits
Spirit of Meekness, Temperance	VS.	spirit of haughtiness (pride)
Galatians 5:22: But the fruit of the Spirit is love, joy, peace, longsuffering, gentleness goodness, faith, Galatians 5:23: Meekness, temperance: against such there is no law.		Proverbs 16:18: Pride goeth before destruction, and an haughty spirit before a fall.

32

Spirit of Truth vs. lying spirit/spirit of error

Holy Spirit and His gifts/fruit	VS.	The other spirits
Spirit of Truth		**lying spirit**
John 16:13: Howbeit when he, the Spirit of truth, is come, he will guide you into all truth: for he shall not speak of himself; but whatsoever he shall hear, that shall he speak: he will shew you things to come.	VS.	**2 Chronicles 18:22:** Now therefore, behold, the LORD hath put a lying spirit in the mouth of these thy prophets, and the LORD hath spoken evil against thee.
		spirit of error
1 John 5:6: This is he that came by water and blood, even Jesus Christ; not by water only, but by water and blood. And it is the Spirit that beareth witness, because the Spirit is truth.		**1 John 4:6:** We are of God: he that knoweth God heareth us; he that is not of God heareth not us. Hereby know we the spirit of truth, and the spirit of error.

33

Spirit of Christ vs. spirit of anti-Christ

Holy Spirit and His gifts/fruit	VS.	The other spirits
Spirit of God/Christ		antichrist spirit
Romans 8:9: But ye are not in the flesh, but in the Spirit, if so be that the Spirit of God dwell in you. Now if any man have not the Spirit of Christ, he is none of his. **1 John 4:2:** Hereby know ye the Spirit of God: Every spirit that confesseth that Jesus Christ is come in the flesh is of God:	VS.	**1 John 4:3:** And every spirit that confesseth not that Jesus Christ is come in the flesh is not of God: and this is the spirit of antichrist, whereof ye have heard it should come; and even now already it is in the world.

Holy Spirit and His gifts/fruit	VS.	The other spirits
Spirit of God/Christ	VS.	antichrist spirit
John 15:26: But when the Comforter is come, whom I will send unto you from the Father, even the Spirit of truth, which proceedeth from the Father, he shall testify of me: **1 Corinthians 12:3:** Wherefore I give you to understand, that no man speaking by the Spirit of God calleth Jesus accursed: and that no man can say that Jesus is the Lord, but by the Holy Ghost.		**1 John 4:3:** And every spirit that confesseth not that Jesus Christ is come in the flesh is not of God: and this is the spirit of antichrist, whereof ye have heard it should come; and even now already it is in the world.

XIII.

The Spirit's Work

34

The Union and the Gift (Graphic)

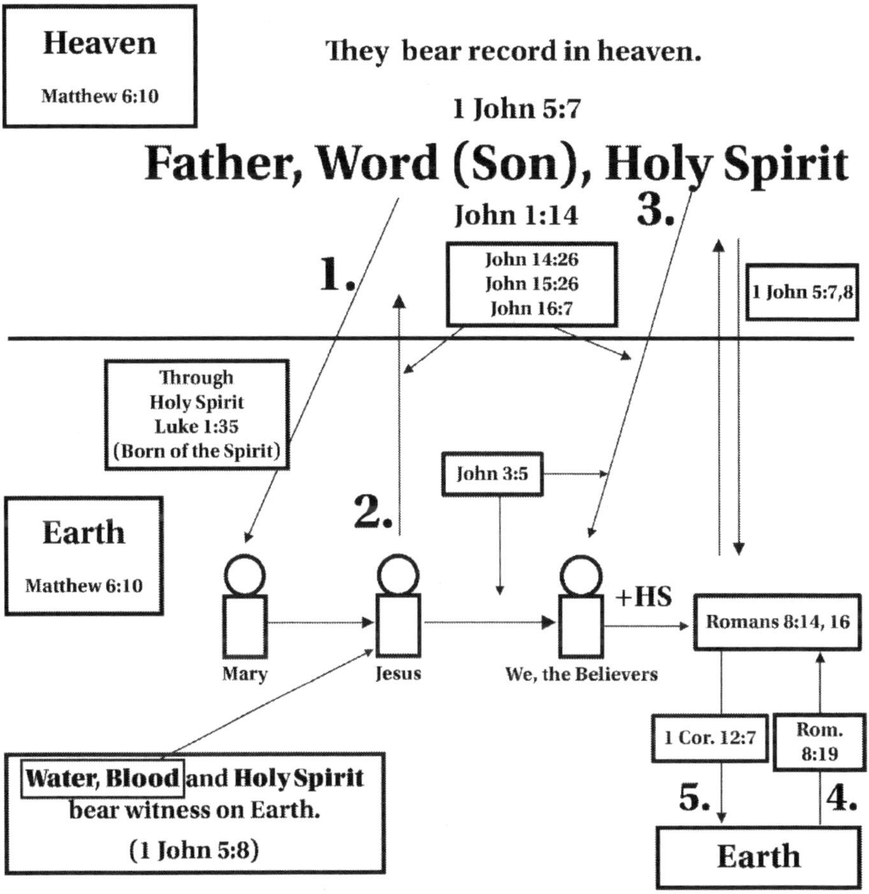

The Holy Spirit:

1. Gave us the One who prepared us and exmplified power (John 14:12)
2. Jesus, in turn, gave us access to the Holy Spirit and access to eternal life.
3. Holy Spirit bearse witness in Heaven, Earth and with our spirits (1 John 5:7, 8 Romans 8:16)
4. Earth cries out for that manifestation that profits every man. (Romans 8:14, 19, 1 Cor 12:17)
5. We should not lack in any gift until the coming of Jesus (1 Cor. 1:7)

35

The Union and the Gift (Scriptures)

Heaven and Earth

Matthew 6:10: Thy kingdom come. Thy will be done in earth, as it is in heaven.

Bear record in Heaven

I John 5:7: For there are three that bear record in heaven, the Father, the Word, and the Holy Ghost: and these three are one.

Word was made flesh

John 1:14: And the Word was made flesh, and dwelt among us, (and we beheld his glory, the glory as of the only begotten of the Father,) full of grace and truth.

Luke 1:35: And the angel answered and said unto her, The Holy Ghost shall come upon thee, and the power of the Highest shall overshadow thee: therefore also that holy thing which shall be born of thee shall be called the Son of God.

Jesus and the gift of Holy Spirit

John 14:26: But the Comforter, which is the Holy Ghost, whom the Father will send in my name, he shall teach you all things, and bring all things to your remembrance, whatsoever I have said unto you.

John 15:26: But when the Comforter is come, whom I will send unto you from the Father, even the Spirit of truth, which proceedeth from the Father, he shall testify of me:

John 16:7: Nevertheless I tell you the truth; It is expedient for you that I go away: for if I go not away, the Comforter will not come unto you; but if I depart, I will send him unto you.

Born of water and the Spirit

John 3:5: Jesus answered, Verily, verily, I say unto thee, Except a man be born of water and of the Spirit, he cannot enter into the kingdom of God.

The Spirit's connection to Heaven and earth

1 John 5:7: For there are three that bear record in heaven, the Father, the Word, and the Holy Ghost: and these three are one.

I John 5:8: And there are three that bear witness in earth, the Spirit, and the water, and the blood: and these three agree in one.

Came by blood and water

1 John 5:6: This is he that came by water and blood, even Jesus Christ; not by water only, but by water and blood. And it is the Spirit that beareth witness, because the Spirit is truth.

The Spirit and the believer

Luke 4:18: The Spirit of the Lord is upon me, because he hath anointed me to preach the gospel to the poor; he hath sent me to heal the broken-hearted, to preach deliverance to the captives, and recovering of sight to the blind, to set at liberty them that are bruised,

Acts 2:38: Then Peter said unto them, Repent, and be baptized every one of you in the name of Jesus Christ for the remission of sins, and ye shall receive the gift of the Holy Ghost.

Acts 2:39: For the promise is unto you, and to your children, and to all that are afar off, even as many as the Lord our God shall call.

The Holy Spirit reveals the believer

Romans 8:14: For as many as are led by the Spirit of God, they are the sons of God.

Romans 8:16: The Spirit itself beareth witness with our spirit, that we are the children of God:

Why the believer and the earth need the Spirit

1 Corinthians 12:7: But the manifestation of the Spirit is given to every man to profit withal.

Romans 8:19: For the earnest expectation of the creature waiteth for the manifestation of the sons of God.

Other Scriptures

John 14:12: Verily, verily, I say unto you, He that believeth on me, the works that I do shall he do also; and greater works than these shall he do; because I go unto my Father.

1 Corinthians 1:7: So that ye come behind in no gift; waiting for the coming of our Lord Jesus Christ:

36

Empowered before the Holy Spirit arrived (Graphic)

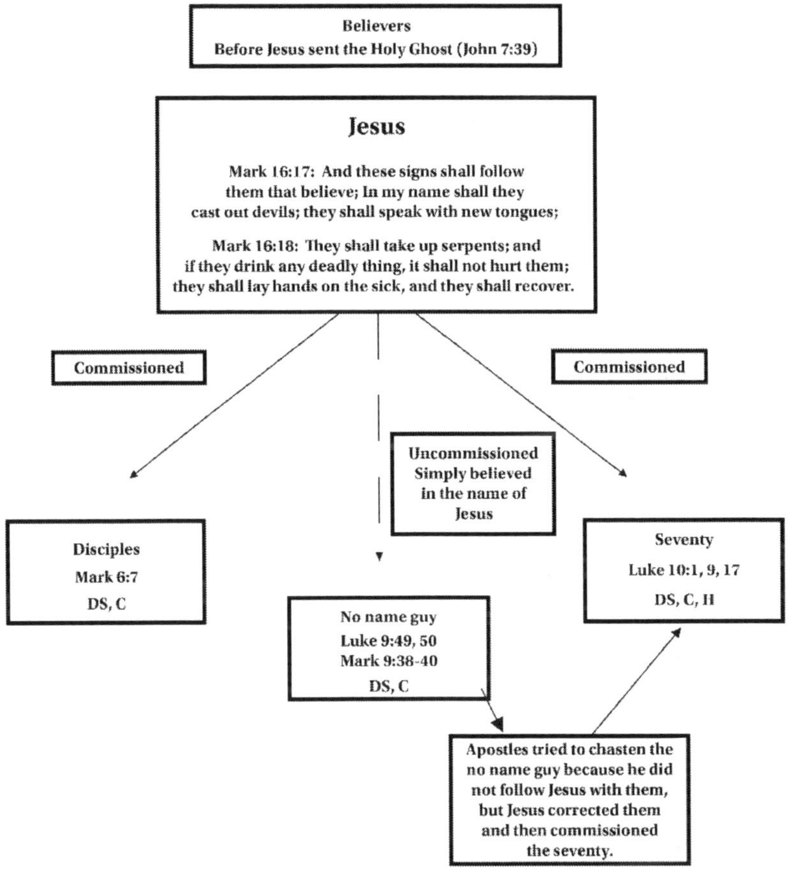

Spiritual Gifts Key (Mark 16:17, 18 and 1 Corinthians 1:7, 8)

Word of Wisdom	W	Prophecy	PR
Word of Knowledge	K	Discerning of spirits	DS
Faith	F	Cast out devils	C
Gifts of Healing	H	Tongues	T
Working of Miracles	M	Interpretation of Tongues	I
Power	PW		

37

Empowered before the Holy Ghost arrived (Scriptures)

The Holy Ghost had not yet been sent

John 7:39: (But this spake he of the Spirit, which they that believe on him should receive: for the Holy Ghost was not yet given; because that Jesus was not yet glorified.)

Jesus empowered the disciples

Mark 6:7: And he called unto him the twelve, and began to send them forth by two and two; and gave them power over unclean spirits;

The "No Name" guy and the name of Jesus

Luke 9:49: And John answered and said, Master, we saw one casting out devils in thy name; and we forbad him, because he followeth not with us.

Luke 9:50: And Jesus said unto him, Forbid him not: for he that is not against us is for us.

Mark 9:38: And John answered him, saying, Master, we saw one casting out devils in thy name, and he followeth not us: and we forbad him, because he followeth not us.

Mark 9:39: But Jesus said, Forbid him not: for there is no man which shall do a miracle in my name, that can lightly speak evil of me.

Mark 9:40: For he that is not against us is on our part.

Jesus empowered the seventy

Luke 10:1: After these things the Lord appointed other seventy also, and sent them two and two before his face into every city and place, whither he himself would come.

Luke 10:9: And heal the sick that are therein, and say unto them, The kingdom of God is come nigh unto you.

Luke 10:17: And the seventy returned again with joy, saying, Lord, even the devils are subject unto us through thy name.

Spiritual gifts key

Mark 16:17: And these signs shall follow them that believe; In my name shall they cast out devils; they shall speak with new tongues;

Mark 16:18: They shall take up serpents; and if they drink any deadly thing, it shall not hurt them; they shall lay hands on the sick, and they shall recover.

1 Corinthians 1:7: So that ye come behind in no gift; waiting for the coming of our Lord Jesus Christ:

1 Corinthians 1:8: Who shall also confirm you unto the end, that ye may be blameless in the day of our Lord Jesus Christ.

38

Empowered after the Holy Spirit arrived (Graphic)

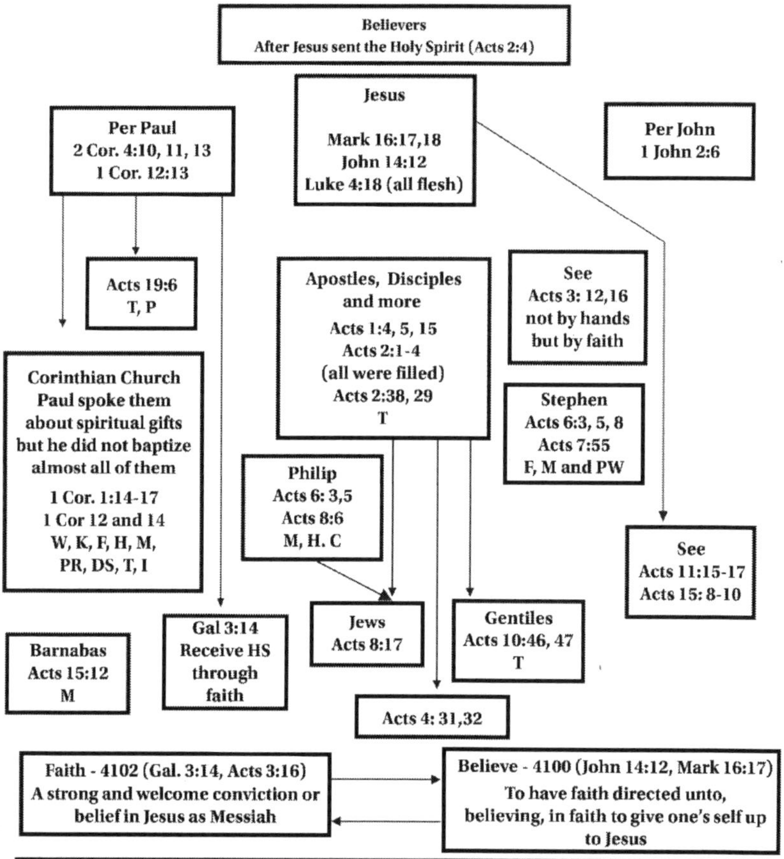

Spiritual Gifts Key (Mark 16:17, 18 and 1 Corinthians 1:7, 8)

Word of Wisdom	W	Prophecy	PR
Word of Knowledge	K	Discerning of spirits	DS
Faith	F	Cast out devils	C
Gifts of Healing	H	Tongues	T
Working of Miracles	M	Interpretation of Tongues	I
Power	PW		

39

Empowered after the Holy Spirit arrived (Scriptures)

Empowerment to His Believers

Acts 2:4: And they were all filled with the Holy Ghost, and began to speak with other tongues, as the Spirit gave them utterance.

Per Jesus

Mark 16:17: And these signs shall follow them that believe; In my name shall they cast out devils; they shall speak with new tongues;

Mark 16:18: They shall take up serpents; and if they drink any deadly thing, it shall not hurt them; they shall lay hands on the sick, and they shall recover.

John 14:12: Verily, verily, I say unto you, He that believeth on me, the works that I do shall he do also; and greater *works* than these shall he do; because I go unto my Father.

Luke 4:18: The Spirit of the Lord *is* upon me, because he hath anointed me to preach the gospel to the poor; he hath sent me to heal the broken-hearted, to preach deliverance to the captives, and recovering of sight to the blind, to set at liberty them that are bruised,

Acts 3:12: And when Peter saw *it,* he answered unto the people, Ye men of Israel, why marvel ye at this? or why look ye so earnestly on us, as though by our own power or holiness we had made this man to walk?

Acts 3:16: And his name through faith in his name hath made this man strong, whom ye see and know: yea, the faith which is by him hath given him this perfect soundness in the presence of you all.

Acts 11:15: And as I began to speak, the Holy Ghost fell on them, as on us at the beginning.

Acts 11:16: Then remembered I the word of the Lord, how that he said, John indeed baptized with water; but ye shall be baptized with the Holy Ghost.

Acts 11:17: Forasmuch then as God gave them the like gift as *he did* unto us, who believed on the Lord Jesus Christ; what was I, that I could withstand God?

Acts 15:8; And God, which knoweth the hearts, bare them witness, giving them the Holy Ghost, even as *he did* unto us;

Acts 15:9: And put no difference between us and them, purifying their hearts by faith.

Acts 15:10: Now therefore why tempt ye God, to put a yoke upon the neck of the disciples, which neither our fathers nor we were able to bear?

Per John

1 John 2:6: He that saith he abideth in him ought himself also so to walk, even as he walked.

Per Paul

2 Corinthians 4:10: Always bearing about in the body the dying of the Lord Jesus, that the life also of Jesus might be made manifest in our body.

2 Corinthians 4:11: For we which live are alway delivered unto death for Jesus' sake, that the life also of Jesus might be made manifest in our mortal flesh.

2 Corinthians 4:13: We having the same spirit of faith, according as it is written, I believed, and therefore have I spoken; we also believe, and therefore speak;

1 Corinthians 12:13: For by one Spirit are we all baptized into one body, whether we be Jews or Gentiles, whether we be bond or free; and have been all made to drink into one Spirit.

Acts 19:6: And when Paul had laid his hands upon them, the Holy Ghost came on them; and they spake with tongues, and prophesied.

1 Corinthians 1:14: I thank God that I baptized none of you, but Crispus and Gaius;

1 Corinthians 1:15: Lest any should say that I had baptized in mine own name.

1 Corinthians 1:16: And I baptized also the household of Stephanas: besides, I know not whether I baptized any other.

1 Corinthians 1:17: For Christ sent me not to baptize, but to preach the gospel: not with wisdom of words, lest the cross of Christ should be made of none effect.

Galatians 3:14: That the blessing of Abraham might come on the Gentiles through Jesus Christ; that we might receive the promise of the Spirit through faith.

1 Corinthians 12 (Spiritual Gifts)

1 Corinthians 12:1: Now concerning spiritual gifts, brethren, I would not have you ignorant.

1 Corinthians 12:2: Ye know that ye were Gentiles, carried away unto these dumb idols, even as ye were led.

1 Corinthians 12:3: Wherefore I give you to understand, that no man speaking by the Spirit of God calleth Jesus accursed: and that no man can say that Jesus is the Lord, but by the Holy Ghost.

1 Corinthians 12:4: Now there are diversities of gifts, but the same Spirit.

1 Corinthians 12:5: And there are differences of administrations, but the same Lord.

1 Corinthians 12:6: And there are diversities of operations, but it is the same God which worketh all in all.

1 Corinthians 12:7: But the manifestation of the Spirit is given to every man to profit withal.

1 Corinthians 12:8: For to one is given by the Spirit the word of wisdom; to another the word of knowledge by the same Spirit;

1 Corinthians 12:9: To another faith by the same Spirit; to another the gifts of healing by the same Spirit;

1 Corinthians 12:10: To another the working of miracles; to another prophecy; to another discerning of spirits; to another divers kinds of tongues; to another the interpretation of tongues:

1 Corinthians 12:11: But all these worketh that one and the selfsame Spirit, dividing to every man severally as he will.

1 Corinthians 12:12: For as the body is one, and hath many members, and all the members of that one body, being many, are one body: so also is Christ.

1 Corinthians 12:13: For by one Spirit are we all baptized into one body, whether we be Jews or Gentiles, whether we be bond or free; and have been all made to drink into one Spirit.

1 Corinthians 12:14: For the body is not one member, but many.

1 Corinthians 12:15: If the foot shall say, Because I am not the hand, I am not of the body; is it therefore not of the body?

1 Corinthians 12:16: And if the ear shall say, Because I am not the eye, I am not of the body; is it therefore not of the body?

1 Corinthians 12:17: If the whole body were an eye, where were the hearing? If the whole were hearing, where were the smelling?

1 Corinthians 12:18: But now hath God set the members every one of them in the body, as it hath pleased him.

1 Corinthians 12:19: And if they were all one member, where were the body?

1 Corinthians 12:20: But now are they many members, yet but one body.

1 Corinthians 12:21: And the eye cannot say unto the hand, I have no need of thee: nor again the head to the feet, I have no need of you.

1 Corinthians 12:22: Nay, much more those members of the body, which seem to be more feeble, are necessary:

1 Corinthians 12:23: And those members of the body, which we think to be less honourable, upon these we bestow more abundant honour; and our uncomely parts have more abundant comeliness.

1 Corinthians 12:24: For our comely parts have no need: but God hath tempered the body together, having given more abundant honour to that part which lacked:

1 Corinthians 12:25: That there should be no schism in the body; but that the members should have the same care one for another.

1 Corinthians 12:26: And whether one member suffer, all the members suffer with it; or one member be honoured, all the members rejoice with it.

1 Corinthians 12:27: Now ye are the body of Christ, and members in particular.

1 Corinthians 12:28: And God hath set some in the church, first apostles, secondarily prophets, thirdly teachers, after that miracles, then gifts of healings, helps, governments, diversities of tongues.

1 Corinthians 12:29: Are all apostles? are all prophets? are all teachers? are all workers of miracles?

1 Corinthians 12:30: Have all the gifts of healing? do all speak with tongues? do all interpret?

1 Corinthians 12:31: But covet earnestly the best gifts: and yet shew I unto you a more excellent way.

1 Corinthians 14 (Prophesying and Tongues)

1 Corinthians 14:1: Follow after charity, and desire spiritual gifts, but rather that ye may prophesy.

1 Corinthians 14:2: For he that speaketh in an unknown tongue speaketh not unto men, but unto God: for no man understandeth him; howbeit in the spirit he speaketh mysteries.

1 Corinthians 14:3: But he that prophesieth speaketh unto men to edification, and exhortation, and comfort.

1 Corinthians 14:4: He that speaketh in an unknown tongue edifieth himself; but he that prophesieth edifieth the church.

1 Corinthians 14:5: I would that ye all spake with tongues, but rather that ye prophesied: for greater is he that prophesieth than he that speaketh with tongues, except he interpret, that the church may receive edifying.

1 Corinthians 14:6: Now, brethren, if I come unto you speaking with tongues, what shall I profit you, except I shall speak to you either by revelation, or by knowledge, or by prophesying, or by doctrine?

1 Corinthians 14:7: And even things without life giving sound, whether pipe or harp, except they give a distinction in the sounds, how shall it be known what is piped or harped?

1 Corinthians 14:8: For if the trumpet give an uncertain sound, who shall prepare himself to the battle?

1 Corinthians 14:9: So likewise ye, except ye utter by the tongue words easy to be understood, how shall it be known what is spoken? for ye shall speak into the air.

1 Corinthians 14:10: There are, it may be, so many kinds of voices in the world, and none of them is without signification.

1 Corinthians 14:11: Therefore if I know not the meaning of the voice, I shall be unto him that speaketh a barbarian, and he that speaketh shall be a barbarian unto me.

1 Corinthians 14:12: Even so ye, forasmuch as ye are zealous of spiritual gifts, seek that ye may excel to the edifying of the church.

1 Corinthians 14:13: Wherefore let him that speaketh in an unknown tongue pray that he may interpret.

1 Corinthians 14:14: For if I pray in an unknown tongue, my spirit prayeth, but my understanding is unfruitful.

1 Corinthians 14:15: What is it then? I will pray with the spirit, and I will pray with the understanding also: I will sing with the spirit, and I will sing with the understanding also.

1 Corinthians 14:16: Else when thou shalt bless with the spirit, how shall he that occupieth the room of the unlearned say Amen at thy giving of thanks, seeing he understandeth not what thou sayest?

1 Corinthians 14:17: For thou verily givest thanks well, but the other is not edified.

1 Corinthians 14:18: I thank my God, I speak with tongues more than ye all:

1 Corinthians 14:19: Yet in the church I had rather speak five words with my understanding, that by my voice I might teach others also, than ten thousand words in an unknown tongue.

1 Corinthians 14:20: Brethren, be not children in understanding: howbeit in malice be ye children, but in understanding be men.

1 Corinthians 14:21: In the law it is written, With men of other tongues and other lips will I speak unto this people; and yet for all that will they not hear me, saith the Lord.

1 Corinthians 14:22: Wherefore tongues are for a sign, not to them that believe, but to them that believe not: but prophesying serveth not for them that believe not, but for them which believe.

1 Corinthians 14:23: If therefore the whole church be come together into one place, and all speak with tongues, and there come in those that are unlearned, or unbelievers, will they not say that ye are mad?

1 Corinthians 14:24: But if all prophesy, and there come in one that believeth not, or one unlearned, he is convinced of all, he is judged of all:

1 Corinthians 14:25: And thus are the secrets of his heart made manifest; and so falling down on his face he will worship God, and report that God is in you of a truth.

1 Corinthians 14:26: How is it then, brethren? when ye come together, every one of you hath a psalm, hath a doctrine, hath a tongue, hath a revelation, hath an interpretation. Let all things be done unto edifying.

1 Corinthians 14:27: If any man speak in an unknown tongue, let it be by two, or at the most by three, and that by course; and let one interpret.

1 Corinthians 14:28: But if there be no interpreter, let him keep silence in the church; and let him speak to himself, and to God.

1 Corinthians 14:29: Let the prophets speak two or three, and let the other judge.

1 Corinthians 14:30: If any thing be revealed to another that sitteth by, let the first hold his peace.

1 Corinthians 14:31: For ye may all prophesy one by one, that all may learn, and all may be comforted.

1 Corinthians 14:32: And the spirits of the prophets are subject to the prophets.

1 Corinthians 14:33: For God is not the author of confusion, but of peace, as in all churches of the saints.

1 Corinthians 14:34: Let your women keep silence in the churches: for it is not permitted unto them to speak; but they are commanded to be under obedience, as also saith the law.

1 Corinthians 14:35: And if they will learn any thing, let them ask their husbands at home: for it is a shame for women to speak in the church.

1 Corinthians 14:36: What? came the word of God out from you? or came it unto you only?

1 Corinthians 14:37: If any man think himself to be a prophet, or spiritual, let him acknowledge that the things that I write unto you are the commandments of the Lord.

1 Corinthians 14:38: But if any man be ignorant, let him be ignorant.

1 Corinthians 14:39: Wherefore, brethren, covet to prophesy, and forbid not to speak with tongues.

1 Corinthians 14:40: Let all things be done decently and in order.

Empowered Apostles, Disciples, and more

Acts 1:4: And, being assembled together with them, commanded them that they should not depart from Jerusalem, but wait for the promise of the Father, which, saith he, ye have heard of me.

Acts 1:5: For John truly baptized with water; but ye shall be baptized with the Holy Ghost not many days hence.

Acts 1:15 : And in those days Peter stood up in the midst of the disciples, and said, (the number of names together were about an hundred and twenty,)

Acts 2:1: And when the day of Pentecost was fully come, they were all with one accord in one place.

Acts 2:2: And suddenly there came a sound from heaven as of a rushing mighty wind, and it filled all the house where they were sitting.

Acts 2:3: And there appeared unto them cloven tongues like as of fire, and it sat upon each of them.

Acts 2:4: And they were all filled with the Holy Ghost, and began to speak with other tongues, as the Spirit gave them utterance.

Acts 2:38: Then Peter said unto them, Repent, and be baptized every one of you in the name of Jesus Christ for the remission of sins, and ye shall receive the gift of the Holy Ghost.

Acts 2:39: For the promise is unto you, and to your children, and to all that are afar off, even as many as the Lord our God shall call.

Acts 4:31: And when they had prayed, the place was shaken where they were assembled together; and they were all filled with the Holy Ghost, and they spake the word of God with boldness.

Acts 4:32: And the multitude of them that believed were of one heart and of one soul: neither said any of them that ought of the things which he possessed was his own; but they had all things common.

Empowered Stephen

Acts 6:3: Wherefore, brethren, look ye out among you seven men of honest report, full of the Holy Ghost and wisdom, whom we may appoint over this business.

Acts 6:5: And the saying pleased the whole multitude: and they chose Stephen, a man full of faith and of the Holy Ghost, and Philip, and Prochorus, and Nicanor, and Timon, and Parmenas, and Nicolas a proselyte of Antioch:

Acts 6:8: And Stephen, full of faith and power, did great wonders and miracles among the people.

Acts 7:55: But he, being full of the Holy Ghost, looked up stedfastly into heaven, and saw the glory of God, and Jesus standing on the right hand of God,

Empowered Phillip

Acts 6:3: Wherefore, brethren, look ye out among you seven men of honest report, full of the Holy Ghost and wisdom, whom we may appoint over this business.

Acts 6:5: And the saying pleased the whole multitude: and they chose Stephen, a man full of faith and of the Holy Ghost, and Philip, and Prochorus, and Nicanor, and Timon, and Parmenas, and Nicolas a proselyte of Antioch:

Acts 8:6: And the people with one accord gave heed unto those things which Philip spake, hearing and seeing the miracles which he did.

Empowered Barnabas

Acts 15:12: Then all the multitude kept silence, and gave audience to Barnabas and Paul, declaring what miracles and wonders God had wrought among the Gentiles by them.

Empowered Jews

Acts 8:17: Then laid they their hands on them, and they received the Holy Ghost.

Empowered Gentiles

Acts 10:46: For they heard them speak with tongues, and magnify God. Then answered Peter,

Acts 10:47: Can any man forbid water, that these should not be baptized, which have received the Holy Ghost as well as we?

Empowered through Faith

Galatians 3:14: That the blessing of Abraham might come on the Gentiles through Jesus Christ; that we might receive the promise of the Spirit through faith.

Acts 3:16: And his name through faith in his name hath made this man strong, whom ye see and know: yea, the faith which is by him hath given him this perfect soundness in the presence of you all.

Empowered through belief

John 14:12: Verily, verily, I say unto you, He that believeth on me, the works that I do shall he do also; and greater works than these shall he do; because I go unto my Father.

Mark 16:17: And these signs shall follow them that believe; In my name shall they cast out devils; they shall speak with new tongues;

Spiritual gifts key

Mark 16:17: And these signs shall follow them that believe; In my name shall they cast out devils; they shall speak with new tongues;

Mark 16:18: They shall take up serpents; and if they drink any deadly thing, it shall not hurt them; they shall lay hands on the sick, and they shall recover.

1 Corinthians 1:7: So that ye come behind in no gift; waiting for the coming of our Lord Jesus Christ:

1 Corinthians 1:8: Who shall also confirm you unto the end, that ye may be blameless in the day of our Lord Jesus Christ.

40

Walk as He walked

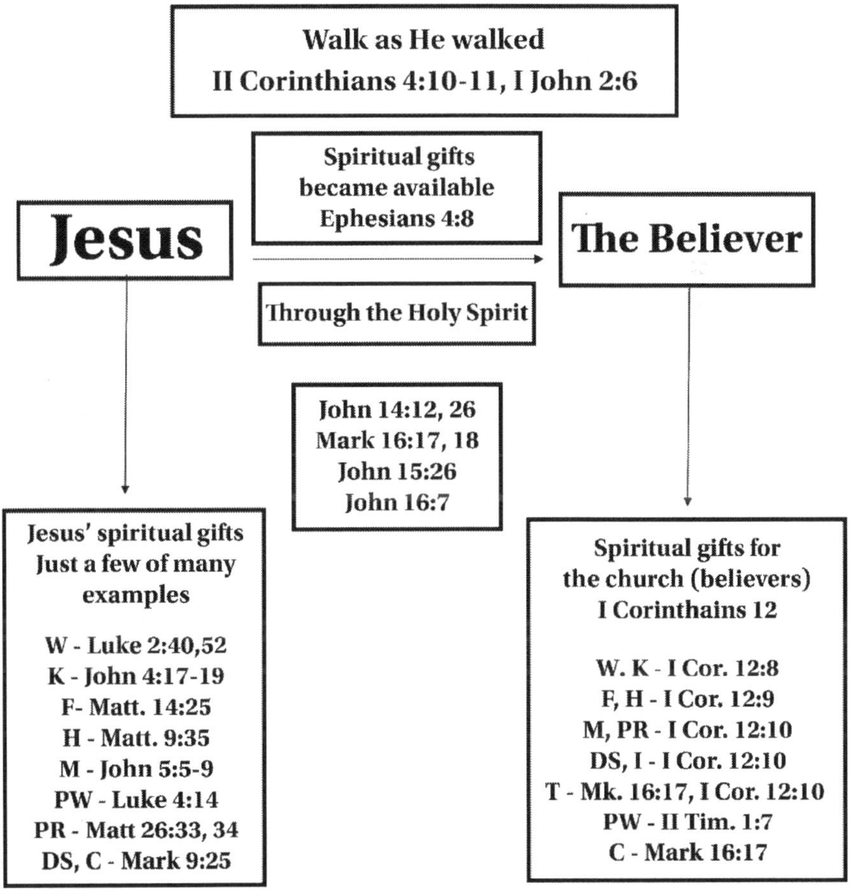

Spiritual Gifts Key (Mark 16:17, 18 and I Corinthians 1:7, 8)

Word of Wisdom	W	Prophecy	PR
Word of Knowledge	K	Discerning of spirits	DS
Faith	F	Cast out devils	C
Gifts of Healing	H	Tongues	T
Working of Miracles	M	Interpretation of Tongues	I
Power	PW		

41

Walk as He walked (Scriptures)

Walk as He walked

2 Corinthians 4:10: Always bearing about in the body the dying of the Lord Jesus, that the life also of Jesus might be made manifest in our body.

2 Corinthians 4:11: For we which live are alway delivered unto death for Jesus' sake, that the life also of Jesus might be made manifest in our mortal flesh.

1 John 2:6: He that saith he abideth in him ought himself also so to walk, even as he walked.

Spiritual gifts became available

Ephesians 4:8: Wherefore he saith, When he ascended up on high, he led captivity captive, and gave gifts unto men.

Jesus' use of spiritual gifts (a few examples)

Word of Wisdom

Luke 2:40: And the child grew, and waxed strong in spirit, filled with wisdom: and the grace of God was upon him.

Luke 2:52: And Jesus increased in wisdom and stature, and in favour with God and man.

Word of Knowledge

Luke 4:17: And there was delivered unto him the book of the prophet Esaias. And when he had opened the book, he found the place where it was written,

Luke 4:18: The Spirit of the Lord is upon me, because he hath anointed me to preach the gospel to the poor; he hath sent me to heal the broken-hearted, to preach deliverance to the captives, and recovering of sight to the blind, to set at liberty them that are bruised,

Luke 4:19: To preach the acceptable year of the Lord.

Faith

Matthew 14:25: And in the fourth watch of the night Jesus went unto them, walking on the sea.

Gifts of Healing

Matthew 9:35: And Jesus went about all the cities and villages, teaching in their synagogues, and preaching the gospel of the kingdom, and healing every sickness and every disease among the people.

Working of Miracles

John 5:5: And a certain man was there, which had an infirmity thirty and eight years.

John 5:6: When Jesus saw him lie, and knew that he had been now a long time in that case, he saith unto him, Wilt thou be made whole?

John 5:7: The impotent man answered him, Sir, I have no man, when the water is troubled, to put me into the pool: but while I am coming, another steppeth down before me.

John 5:8: Jesus saith unto him, Rise, take up thy bed, and walk.

John 5:9: And immediately the man was made whole, and took up his bed, and walked: and on the same day was the sabbath.

Power

Luke 4:14: And Jesus returned in the power of the Spirit into Galilee: and there went out a fame of him through all the region round about.

Prophecy

Matthew 26:33: Peter answered and said unto him, Though all men shall be offended because of thee, yet will I never be offended.

Matthew 26:34: Jesus said unto him, Verily I say unto thee, That this night, before the cock crow, thou shalt deny me thrice.

Discerning of spirits

Mark 9:25: When Jesus saw that the people came running together, he rebuked the foul spirit, saying unto him, Thou dumb and deaf spirit, I charge thee, come out of him, and enter no more into him.

Cast out devils

Mark 9:25: When Jesus saw that the people came running together, he rebuked the foul spirit, saying unto him, Thou dumb and deaf spirit, I charge thee, come out of him, and enter no more into him.

Spiritual gifts for the church

Word of wisdom

1 Corinthians 12:8: For to one is given by the Spirit the word of wisdom; to another the word of knowledge by the same Spirit;

Word of knowledge

1 Corinthians 12:8: For to one is given by the Spirit the word of wisdom; to another the word of knowledge by the same Spirit;

Faith

1 Corinthians 12:9: To another faith by the same Spirit; to another the gifts of healing by the same Spirit;

Gifts of healing

1 Corinthians 12:9: To another faith by the same Spirit; to another the gifts of healing by the same Spirit;

Working of Miracles

1 Corinthians 12:10: To another the working of miracles; to another prophecy; to another discerning of spirits; to another divers kinds of tongues; to another the interpretation of tongues:

Prophecy

1 Corinthians 12:10: To another the working of miracles; to another prophecy; to another discerning of spirits; to another divers kinds of tongues; to another the interpretation of tongues:

Discerning of spirits

1 Corinthians 12:10: To another the working of miracles; to another prophecy; to another discerning of spirits; to another divers kinds of tongues; to another the interpretation of tongues:

Interpretation of Tongues

1 Corinthians 12:10: To another the working of miracles; to another prophecy; to another discerning of spirits; to another divers kinds of tongues; to another the interpretation of tongues:

Tongues

Mark 16:17: And these signs shall follow them that believe; In my name shall they cast out devils; they shall speak with new tongues;

1 Corinthians 12:10: To another the working of miracles; to another prophecy; to another discerning of spirits; to another divers kinds of tongues; to another the interpretation of tongues:

Power

2 Timothy 1:7: For God hath not given us the spirit of fear; but of power, and of love, and of a sound mind.

Cast out devils

Mark 16:17: And these signs shall follow them that believe; In my name shall they cast out devils; they shall speak with new tongues;

XIV.

GO FORTH AND CONQUER...

42

Go forth and conquer... (letter)

Dear Friends in Christ:

Power. We serve a God who gives us not a spirit of fear, but a Spirit of power (II Timothy 1:7).

We have access to this Spirit. I wrote this book because I wanted everyone reading it to know just how awesome, available and accessible He is. I encourage you to keep a copy of this book with you and use it as a guide to learn more about the Holy Spirit. Use it during your studies and use it when you pray. Use it for the moments when you minister to or share with someone. Use it when you thank Him for being with you.

The Holy Spirit is a gentle Spirit. Since He is tender (and powerful), He can only do what He does best when there is an invitation. Should this invitation come only at the time of receiving the gift of tongues? No. As He is so much more than just the gift of tongues, you should invite Him to guide you throughout your day, in every circumstance, in every interaction, in every church service, on your job, in your home, in your marriage, and your relationships. When you are down, you should invite the Spirit to comfort you and give you hope. Ask the Holy Spirit to impart kindness, temperance, love, joy, peace and everything else that He has to offer.

As we continuously seek these gifts in our lives, we ask him for impartations around every turn. We need Him to help us serve our fellow man in the natural world and in the supernatural. Do you need to go against the devil and his army? The sons of Sceva (Acts 19:11-16) would probably recommend that you do not do so without the Spirit in and around you. As this passage illustrates, we need to know the Holy Spirit for ourselves because that is how the enemy will know who we are.

He is such a gift, and I get so excited when I talk about Him and when I engage Him. I love Him so much, and I hope that this book inspires you to find out everything you can about the Spirit. As I mentioned before, the Holy Spirit is not someone who only operates in leadership. He is a Spirit who needs and desires willing vessels regardless of who you are, what you look like, or how long you have been in Christ. He merely needs entry and a passion for letting Him guide you.

I pray that you enjoyed my book, *Yours Truly, The Holy Spirit* because the Holy Spirit is truly yours with every invitation. I pray that you engage Him in every moment and that you walk through Him. He is our direct connection to heaven, and as God speaks, the Spirit relays. Remember that the Holy Spirit is always ready and waiting to work through you—He is just waiting for you and your 24/7/365 day open-door policy.

God bless all of you and with the Holy Spirit, go forth and conquer.

Your friend in Christ,
Marco

About the Author

Marco Harris is man of God with passions for the Holy Spirit, spiritual warfare, and intimate worship. His primary mission scripture is Isaiah 61:1 and he hopes that this book will give you, the reader, the fuel you need to start your fire. He and his family reside in Richmond, Virginia.

https://www.mhkreates.com
https://www.facebook.com/mhkreates

Another Favorite Scripture

Jeremiah 33:3

Call unto me, and I will answer thee, and shew thee great and mighty things, which thou knowest not.

Made in the USA
Columbia, SC
04 July 2025

60338936R00120